Beyond Doubt

*How to Be Sure
of Your Salvation*

Shawn Lazar

Beyond Doubt

How to Be Sure of Your Salvation

Shawn Lazar

Grace Evangelical Society
Denton, Texas 76202

Dedicated to Mom and Nanny,
who introduced me to Jesus.

Contents

Are You Baffled by Belief?

THERE I WAS, complaining again. "Do you know what really surprises me? All the Christians I talk to who aren't sure they're saved."

"That's my problem!" my friend blurted out.

"Really?"

"Yes, and it's really wearing me out," he continued. "No matter how hard I pray, I'm still not sure if I'm saved."

I was shocked.

I had known Rich and his family for several years. They went to a Bible church. Their pastor graduated from Dallas Seminary. They home-schooled. They were serious, conscientious, Christians. Rich read Christian books, and often debated theology. I never would have guessed he struggled with doubts about his salvation.

"But don't you believe in Jesus?" I asked.

"Yes, I do."

"And you believe in justification by faith, apart from works, right?"

"Yes, I believe that, too," he said.

"So how can you doubt that you're saved?"

"Well, I believe those things," Rich said, "but I don't know if I *really* believe them."

Uh oh.

I had heard that before. "*Really* believe" as opposed to just "believe." I could guess what happened. I had seen it hundreds of times. Someone told Rich there were different *kinds* of faith—different ways of believing the same saving message—and he wasn't sure if he had the right kind.

"What do you think the difference is between 'believe' and 'really believe'?" I asked.

"I know I have *head* faith, but I don't know if I have *heart* faith," he struggled.

"How are those two things different? How is believing that Jesus justifies us by faith apart from works different if you believe it with your 'heart' rather than your 'head'"?

"I don't know! That's the whole problem. If I knew what the difference was, I'd do something about it. Maybe it feels different? Or maybe if you really believe something with all your heart you're supernaturally motivated by that belief? If I really believed, wouldn't I sin less, or do more good? I just don't know."

"Did you ask your pastor about it?"

"Yes. He said, 'Give me twenty years, and I'll probably be able to tell if you're really a Christian based on the fruits of your life.' So, I guess it's wait-and-see. But for now, I don't know."

That was a heart-breaking conversation.

It's unnatural for a Christian to live in doubt about his salvation.

If you had children, would you want them to never be sure if they're really your children? Or would you want your kids to doubt whether you loved them?

Of course not.

It's the same with God. He wants you to be assured of His Word and His promises. He wants you to know that He is your Father and you are His child, and that by faith in Jesus, you'll live with Him forever.

Doubt is *not* God's will for you.

Can you know beyond all doubt that you are saved? Yes, you *can* and yes, you *should*!

This book will explore some common errors about faith and salvation that prevent people like you from having assurance.

If you're doubting your salvation, I want to encourage you. I believe that you can believe. I have no doubt that you can believe beyond a doubt. I'm sure that you can be assured.

As Jesus said, "This is the work of God, that you believe in Him whom He has sent" (John 6:29).

It's God's will for you.

It's Jesus' will for you.
You can banish doubt forever.
I'll prove it to you from the Bible.

CHAPTER 1

Don't Ask Jesus Into Your Heart: The Error of a Confusing Gospel

DID YOU UNDERSTAND the gospel the first time you heard it?

I surely didn't.

I sporadically attended a Bible church for nearly five years before it ever clicked for me.

I don't know why I didn't understand it right away. Was it because I was too young? Was it because I wasn't spiritually ready to hear it? Did no one ever explain the saving message to me in a way that I could understand? Did the preachers use vague "Christianese" that left me in a mental fog? Was I confused because I only ever heard a confusing message?

Maybe that's your problem, too. If you doubt your salvation, it could be because you have only ever heard a confusing message. It happens more often than you think. It reminds me of something that recently happened to a pastor friend of mine.

Muddled Mystical Missionaries

A young missionary who wanted to raise support recently contacted my pastor friend. He didn't know her and she didn't know the church, so they met to discuss what she believed about the gospel and how she would share it with others.

It didn't go well.

"Tell me about yourself," he said.

"Well, I was raised in a Christian family," she began. "And although I was baptized at summer camp, I only gave my life to Christ five years ago. That's when the Lord really touched my heart. I just felt His special presence, which was so amazing. Now I have a passion to reach the lost with the gospel. I believe the Lord wants me in the mission field."

"So you know you are saved because you gave your life to Christ five years ago and had some sort of encounter?"

"Yes! It was so amazing."

"And how do you share the good news with unbelievers? What's the message you tell them?"

"I tell them about Jesus being the Son of God, how He died on the cross for sin, so if anyone receives Him into their hearts they will go to heaven."

"I see," the pastor said. "I'm sorry, but we can't support you."

"What?" The missionary was shocked. "Why not?"

"Because that's not what we believe."

"It isn't? Isn't this a Bible church? Aren't you Evangelicals?"

"Yes it is, and we are."

"So, what's wrong?"

"The problem is," my friend began to explain, "what you just shared is very confusing. It's not a clear saving message. We only support missionaries who share the gospel clearly."

Before we take a closer look at what that missionary said, did you notice anything unclear in her testimony?

If you were an unbeliever hearing about Christianity for the first time, would you think that her message was clear?

How about some other popular "evangelistic" phrases?

- "If you want to be saved, you need to ask Jesus into your heart."
- "If you want to know the Lord, then won't you come forward today?"
- "You can go to heaven if you just say this Sinner's Prayer."
- "If you want to be saved you need to believe in Jesus with your heart, not just your

head."
- "It isn't enough to just mentally believe in Him, you also have to trust Him!"

Haven't we all heard altar calls like this? Maybe you've even shared one with an unbeliever. Do you think they're clear?

I don't.

Think Like a Kid

Having three kids under 5 has made me very self-aware of how I explain the things of God to them. So imagine if you told a little girl to ask Jesus into her heart. How would she understand that?

She would think that Jesus must be very small to fit inside a heart.

Or she might think Jesus is like Santa Clause, able to magically slide down very narrow places.

She would probably wonder what it felt like to have Jesus in her heart. After all, it would feel like something, wouldn't it? But what? She wouldn't be sure. If she asked Jesus in, but didn't feel anything, she might wonder if she did something wrong. She might ask Jesus to come in again and again, just to be sure.

If she did feel something, but later lost that feeling, she would wonder if she had done something to upset Jesus to make Him leave her heart. She'd wonder why Jesus didn't love her like the other kids in church. She might doubt that she was really saved at all.

And then, after years of seeking an experience, but never having one, after years of deviating between faith and doubt, the grown-up child, who never heard a clear gospel message, and who never had assurance, might give up on Christianity altogether.

The Reason Why It Is Confusing

Back to the missionary and my pastor friend. Why did he say her message was unclear?

Well, compare her evangelistic message with one from Jesus' own ministry.

The Gospel According to John tells us how Jesus evangelized. In John 3, the Lord was having a conversation about how to be born again with a Pharisee named Nicodemus. Nicodemus didn't know how to be born again. In fact, he had never even heard of the concept, let alone understand it. So Jesus told him:

> "For God so loved the world that He gave His only begotten Son, that whoever believes in Him should not perish but have everlasting life" (John 3:16).

So simple. So clear. So powerful.

If you *believe* in Jesus, you *have everlasting life*, and you *won't perish*. Ever.

It's that simple.

So why was the missionary's message unclear? Because it didn't explain any of those essential elements of the message of life.

First, she didn't explain what we are supposed to do: *believe in Jesus*.

Second, she didn't explain what we are believing in Jesus for: *everlasting life*.

Third, she didn't explain when we get eternal life: *believers have it as a present possession*.

Fourth, she didn't explain that what we get is permanent: *believers shall never perish*.

In other words, the young missionary didn't make *any* part of the saving message clear.

What she presented might be common ways of talking about evangelism today, but it's Christianese. It's not Biblical. It's not how Jesus did evangelism. And it's very vague compared to Jesus' simple message.

Yes, the missionary spoke about giving her life to Christ and receiving Him into her heart, but that is not the same, and not as clear, as simply telling people to *believe in Jesus*.

In fact, many people think that "giving your life to Christ" means having to do good works to be saved. Many think "receiving Jesus into your heart" means having a dramatic mystical experience.

The missionary also wanted people to believe that Jesus is the Son of God. That's good. He *is* the Son of God. But you can believe that *and also believe in salvation by works.* Actually, you can believe that Jesus is the Son of God and have no idea that there is such a thing as salvation at all.

She spoke about going to heaven. That's good. Believers *will* go to heaven (at least, for a while, until God creates the new earth). But you can believe that and deny (or not know) that everlasting life is a present possession, something Jesus gives us at the moment of faith. Countless Christians have no idea that they have eternal life right now. Instead, they only hope they'll be saved sometime in the future. But that's not what Jesus told Nicodemus to believe.

The missionary wanted the lost to feel Jesus' special presence. I agree, the Christian life should be one of joy and abundance. But someone could be full of good feelings and yet also falsely think that eternal salvation can be won or lost based on your works.

Do you see the problem now?

What the missionary said wasn't necessarily *wrong*, but it wasn't *evangelistic.*

In fact, she left out all the essential elements of an evangelistic message. That's why my pastor friend could not support her.

Jesus Is Our Model

When we don't share a clear gospel message

in simple language, the result can be disastrous. Generations of Christians are left confused about the only condition for eternal salvation. And since they never know what the condition is, they can't believe it, or be sure if they've ever met it.

Instead of *assurance*, they have *doubts*.

Terrible, tormenting doubts.

If the lost are going to meet God in eternity, they'll need clear directions. They need to be told *exactly* what they must do to be saved. Instead of vague Christianese, they need to be told, in no uncertain terms, to *believe in Jesus for everlasting life that cannot be lost*.

Is that why you doubt your salvation? Have you only ever heard, and believed, an unclear saving message?

Will you believe Jesus' promise of life now?

CHAPTER 2

Are You Good Enough? *The Error of Salvation by Works*

MOM WAS A life-long smoker. She started in her early teens and smoked multiple packs a day.

When my siblings and I were growing up, we knew smoking was dangerous. We saw the educational videos, the graphic commercials, and the photos of smoker's lungs. We knew smoking was deadly and asked Mom to quit. Actually, we *begged* her to quit. Over the years she tried many times, but it never stuck.

And then, during the summer of 2012 Mom's health took a turn for the worse. She started losing a lot of weight. My sister (who lived with her) called me and said Mom hadn't eaten any solid food for a couple of weeks.

So I got Mom on the phone and asked her

what was going on.

"It's only a sore throat," she said in a raspy voice. "A little broth and I'll be fine in a couple of weeks."

"Mom, it's probably cancer. You need to see a doctor."

"It's not cancer. It's just a cold. Don't you worry about it."

Well, as summer went by, Mom's condition got progressively worse until she looked like a skeleton. We kept begging her to go to the hospital, but she refused. By August, that "sore throat" still hadn't gone away and she was getting weaker by the day. Mom finally consented to see a doctor, and as soon as she walked into his office, he sent her to the nearest ER. After a battery of tests, the doctors confirmed Mom had cancer.

It was everywhere.

In her throat, lungs, stomach, and lymph nodes.

Terminal.

The family was sad at the news, but we weren't surprised. We all saw it coming from miles away.

But not Mom.

She was in shock. I mean, genuine, never-saw-it-coming shock.

You might find that hard to believe.

You would think she knew the truth all along. Any rational person could read the signs—every time she looked in the mirror, checked her weight, tried to swallow. But the human capacity for self-deception is astounding. Mom honestly didn't think she was that sick. A cold maybe. Or a scratchy throat. But not cancer. And certainly nothing *terminal.*

Sadly, four months later she died.

Sinners are like my mother. "I'm fine," they say., "Don't you worry about me." They're in denial about their spiritual condition.

When you tell them the bad news they're sinners who can't save themselves, they don't believe you. They think they're basically good people, with a few foibles, but God will understand, and let them into heaven anyway. In other words, they believe in salvation by works.

Is that what *you* believe?

And here's another question. If that's what you believe, *do you have assurance of salvation?*

I find that people who believe in salvation by works have *hopes* of being saved, but never *certainty*.

If that sounds like you, the Bible offers help, but it'll sting a little.

The Purpose of the Law

You want to do good, be good, and live for God.

That's good.

But you also expect to be *saved* on the basis of being a good person.

That's not so good.

In fact, that's very bad.

Are you really saved by doing good? Is that what the Bible teaches? The Apostle Paul wrestled with this question and received a surprising answer from the Lord:

> Man is not justified by the works of the law but by faith in Jesus Christ...for by the works of the law no flesh shall be justified (Galatians 2:16).

Let's be crystal clear about what Paul is saying here. No human being will be justified by doing works of the law. No one.

Not Paul.

Not me.

And not you, either.

If you're expecting to be saved based on your good works, I can already tell you how that story is going to end.

So why did God give us the Law? Why did He command us to do good, and to love our neighbors?

On the one hand, it's because our neighbors need our help. The commands aren't there so we can earn eternal life, but so that we'll know how to help the people around us.

But on the other hand, and more to the point, it has to do with human psychology and our stubborn refusal to recognize the depths of our own

sin. Just as Mom needed a lab test to convince her
she had cancer, God often needs to shake us out
of our self-delusions about being basically good.
So He gave us the Law. It's our spiritual lab test.
Here's how Paul explained it:

> The knowledge of sin comes through the
> law (Romans 3:20, HCSB).

> Moreover the law entered that the offense
> might abound. But where sin abounded,
> grace abounded much more (Romans
> 5:20).

> What shall we say, then? Is the law sinful?
> Certainly not! Nevertheless, I would not
> have known what sin was had it not been
> for the law (Romans 7:7).

> Why then was the law given? It was added
> because of transgressions until the Seed
> to whom the promise was made would
> come. The law was put into effect through
> angels by means of a mediator (Galatians
> 3:19, HCSB).

Did you get that?

Is it clear why God gave us the Law?

It isn't meant to give you a pat on the back for
being a good person. On the contrary, it's supposed to give you smack on the conscience, show-

ing you that you're a bad person! The Law is there, not to remind you how good your are, but to reveal your sin so there will be no doubt in your mind about where you stand with God.

The Law commands and convicts. It points a finger straight at you and loudly says, "You failed!"

It's like a lab test that proves you have cancer.

Don't Settle for Knockoffs

Of course, not every lab test is accurate. Some are knockoffs of the real thing, or skewed to give you the result you want. Many churches do that with the Law. They preach a knock-off, what I call "Cheap Law."

God's Law demands perfection.

Cheap Law asks for your best shot.

God's Law sets the bar as high as His glory (Romans 3:23).

Cheap Law sets the bar low.

Very low.

A religions that teach Cheap Law have to set the bar low, don't they? After all, if you want to convince people they can be saved by doing good works, those works have to be attainable. If it was too hard, they'd be discouraged and give up. So instead of perfection, all they demand is:

"Just get baptized."

"Come to Communion at least twice a year."

"Say 10 prayers, 5 times a day."

"Try to be a good person."

"Do your best and God will do the rest."

You've heard those things before, haven't you? It makes it seem as though God isn't asking all that much of you and me. "Hey, I can do that," people think. And that's the point.

But does God really demand that little?

Is the bar really that low?

Does God preach Cheap Law?

No.

Not even close.

Here's what God says the Law actually demands (emphasis added):

> "For I am Yahweh your God, so you must consecrate yourselves and *be holy* because I am holy" (Leviticus 11:44, HCSB, emphasis added).

> "Speak to the entire Israelite community and tell them: '*Be holy* because I, Yahweh your God, am holy'" (Leviticus 19:2, HCSB, emphasis added).

> "You shall be *blameless* before the Lord your God" (Deuteronomy 18:13, HCSB, emphasis added).

> "Therefore *you are to be perfect*, as your heavenly Father is perfect" (Matthew 5:48,

NASB, emphasis added).

Holy. Blameless. Perfect. Now do you understand what God expects of you? You have to be
holy, just as He is, blameless, just as He is, perfect,
absolutely perfect, and nothing less will do.

How do you measure up to *that* standard?

Are you beginning to see that your only hope
of salvation lies in God's mercy, not in your efforts
at fulfilling a Cheap Law?

And where has God chosen to show you
mercy?

There's only one place—through His Son, Jesus
Christ.

As Alan Redpath said, "God has nothing for
any one of us except we find it in the Lord Jesus
Christ."[1]

You don't get to choose where God shows you
mercy. It's found in Jesus, or not at all.

Which brings me back to why you may lack
assurance.

If you believe that salvation depends on keeping up some level of good behavior, instead of
simply believing in Jesus, then you'll never have
assurance, because you'll always doubt that you've
been good enough in the past, present or future,
to be saved.

And when you realize what God really demands—holiness, blamelessness, perfection—
you'll *know* that you're not good enough, and
you'll *never* have assurance.

What Now?

If you lack assurance because you believe in *salvation by works,* then the solution to your problem is quite simple: believe in *salvation by faith*!

It's a simple message, but so many find it hard to accept because we're hard-wired to think we have to work for all the important things in life. Consequently, it's hard to get people to even *consider* the faith message, let alone *believe* it.

When someone asked Jesus, "What shall we do, that we may work the works of God?" The Lord gave an ironic answer. "This is the work of God, *that you believe in Him whom He sent*" (John 6:28-29, emphasis added).

People are always looking around for new ways to save themselves by works. Jesus had the hardest time getting across the message that *works are not a condition of salvation.* Faith is the *only* condition.

Do you want to work the works of God? Then believe in Jesus for eternal life.

And what do believers have? "He who hears My word and believes in Him who sent Me *has everlasting life,* and shall not come into judgment, but has passed from death into life" (John 5:24).

That's "has," present tense.

What's the significance of the present tense? It means if you believe you *have* everlasting life as a present possession.

It's already yours!

There's nothing more to do!

No church or priest can dangle the goal of everlasting life, if only you do this, that, or the other thing.

If you believe in Jesus for it, you already have it, no works required.

Will you doubt Jesus or believe Him?

Endnotes

1. Alan Redpath, *Victorious Christian Living: Studies in the Book of Joshua* (London: Pickering and Inglis, 1955), 22.

CHAPTER 3

A Back-Loaded Gospel:
The Error of Redefining Faith

MY COLLEGE ROOMMATE had a talent for card tricks.

It infuriated me.

He had this one trick called The Slapstick.

First, he'd shuffle a deck of cards and ask me to pick one without showing him. After I had memorized it and put it back into the deck, he'd shuffle the cards again and place the deck between my fingers. And then— wham!—he'd slap my hand sending the cards scattered across the floor.

All except one.

There, in my hand, I'd still be holding the card I originally picked out of the deck!

How'd he do it?

As I said, it infuriated me!

I wasn't angry at my roommate—his trick was great—I was frustrated because I wasn't clever enough to figure out how he did it. Somehow, he tricked me. I missed his sleight of hand.

Unfortunately, too many preachers play sleight of hand with the gospel.

With one hand they distract you with talk about justification by faith alone, making you comfortable. And then—wham!—with the other hand they sneak in salvation by works while you're not paying attention.

They "back-load" the gospel.

What does that mean?

Sneaking in Works

A preacher *front-loads* the gospel when he teaches that you are saved by faith *plus* works.

A preacher *back-loads* the gospel when he teaches we are saved by faith *that* works.

See the difference?

Or rather, do you see there really is no difference?

Front-loading the gospel *openly* makes works a condition of salvation.

Back-loading the gospel *covertly* makes works a condition of salvation, by subtly redefining faith to include works.

People who believe in a back-loaded gospel lack assurance for the same reason people who believe in salvation by works lack assurance. They need to look at their works to know if they "really" believe. But since they're all sinners, with a mixture of good and bad behavior, they're never sure if they're good enough to be saved.

Do *you* believe a back-loaded gospel?

Redefining Faith

Let me give you an example of the kind of sleight-of-hand I have in mind, where teachers initially claim to believe in justification by faith apart from works, only to introduce works through the back-door, by redefining faith to include works.

In a recently published *Systematic Theology*, a Calvinistic author claims to believe in justification by faith apart from works. As he writes,

> Justification is by faith apart from works, apart from works of the law, without works.[1]

This is admirably clear, is it not? Three times in one sentence he emphasizes that justification is by faith apart from works. If you heard him preach that, you'd think he believed it!

The author even rightly recognizes that if justification were based even partly on works, we could not have assurance. In discussing the Roman Catholic view, he says,

This means, then, that salvation is based partly on our works. The consequence, then, is that we cannot be assured of our salvation in this life, because we are never sure whether our works have been sufficient.[2]

So, if you were to hear this man teach about justification from the pulpit, you would come away thinking he believed in justification by faith, apart from works.

And you would be wrong.

Read on a little further and you find he plays sleight of hand with the saving message and redefines faith to include doing good works:

> …saving faith is a *faith that works*…[3]

> …justification is by a living faith, not a dead faith, *a faith that works*, rather than a mere profession. But faith does not justify because of its connection to works. It justifies because its nature is to trust, in this case to trust the grace of God in Christ. That trust motivates us to please God *and therefore to do good works.*[4]

> …if you assent to the truths of Scripture, not feebly or forgetfully, *but in a way that determines your behavior, thoughts, and feelings*, then it seems to me that you have

all that is needed for true faith. But then
your faith is better described not merely
as assent, but according to the third com-
ponent of faith, trust.[5]

The author goes on to explain that one of the
components of trust is "subjection to Christ as
Lord, a willingness to obey…faith must be living
faith, *obedient faith, faith that works…*"[6]

On the one hand, this man will teach you are
saved by faith, apart from works.

On the other hand, if you don't have works
you don't really believe and aren't saved.

Confused yet?

What exactly is the difference?

Whether you are saved by faith *plus* works or
by faith *that* works, either way, works are made a
condition of salvation. And if it's a condition of
salvation, we can never have assurance. As the author himself admitted, "we are never sure whether
our works have been sufficient."

That is the result of the back-loaded gospel.

Works Don't Work

If you have become confused by a back-loaded
gospel, the only solution is to clearly understand
that salvation is by faith apart from works, period!
No tricks. No fine print. No reservations.

John's Gospel tells us the result of believing in
Jesus is that we get eternal life (cf. John 3:16; 3:36;

5:24; 6:47; 10:28). It never ever says that salvation depends on works. It only ever says that salvation is by faith. The verb *believe* is mentioned one hundred times. No wonder John's Gospel has been called "The Gospel of Belief."

Paul, in his letters to the Galatians and Romans, is even more explicit. He repeatedly proclaims that we are justified by faith apart from doing the good works of the law.

Remember the verses we quoted above?

> Therefore, having been justified by faith, we have peace with God through our Lord Jesus Christ (Romans 5:1).

> For by grace you have been saved through faith, and that not of yourselves; it is the gift of God, not of works, lest anyone should boast (Ephesians 2:8-9).

> Not by works of righteousness which we have done, but according to His mercy He saved us (Titus 3:5a).

> Knowing that a man is not justified by the works of the law but by faith in Jesus Christ, even we have believed in Christ Jesus, that we might be justified by faith in Christ and not by the works of the law; for by the works of the law no flesh shall be

justified (Galatians 2:16).

Does it get any clearer than that?

We are saved through believing in Jesus, not by doing the good works of the Law. If doing good works was part of what it means to believe, Paul's argument would fall apart.

But they're not the same. Faith and works are polar opposites.

To believe means to be persuaded that something is true. It contains no element of behavior. No work. Of course, our beliefs *influence* our behavior, but you can't say that works are part of faith itself.

Faith and works are two different things, and faith is the *only* condition of salvation.

Is that why you lack assurance?

Were you taught that works were part of faith? Were you taught that you didn't really believe unless you acted a certain way? Were you confused by a back-loaded gospel?

In that case, instead of believing the back-loaded gospel, believe Jesus' promise that we are saved by simply believing in Him. Let that be your only ground for assurance.

Endnotes

1. John M. Frame, *Systematic Theology: An Introduction to Christian Belief* (Philipsburg, NJ: P&R Publishing, 2013), 970

2. Ibid., 969, emphasis added.
3. Ibid., 970, emphasis added.
4. Ibid, emphasis added.
5. Ibid., 952-53, emphasis added.
6. Ibid. He incorrectly quotes James 2:14-26 as proof of his position. See chapter 8 for the correct interpretation of that passage as it relates to faith.

CHAPTER 4

Can You Lose Eternal Life?
The Error of Probation Salvation

IMAGINE IF YOU lived in the witness protection program. You saw a major crime, could identify who committed it, and those criminals were now threatening your life if you testified against them. So the US Marshalls gave you a new name, a new identity, and a new life.

But there's a price to pay.

If you go into witness protection, you'll spend the rest of your life in fear, never knowing if you'll be safe. You'll always wonder if the mob has someone looking for you, right this very moment. You'll never know if someone is waiting just around the corner, ready to kill you.

Would you feel secure under those conditions?

Would you live your life in peace?

Or would you be constantly walking on egg-shells, wondering if somehow, someday, the mob would finally get you?

Of course you would live in fear. Your whole life would be lived under the shadow of a giant question mark—"Will I make it?"

That's the same struggle many people have with salvation.

Instead of believing they have eternal life and will never perish (as Jesus promised), they believe they can lose their salvation at any moment. If they get out of line—sin, doubt, fail to do good—God will take their salvation away. Instead of be-lieving Jesus' promise of secure salvation (i.e., that believers "shall never perish"), they believe in pro-bation salvation (i.e., "you're saved for now...").

Is that your struggle?

Do you lack assurance, because you think you could lose your salvation at any moment?

If so, let's take a closer look at Jesus' promise of eternal life. I want you to have no doubt that Jesus promised security, not probation.

Probation Salvation?

Here is a typical quote expressing the idea that salvation is probationary. You might have heard something like this in your church:

> The believer is still in a state of probation. If he were not liable to fall, he would not

be in a probationary, but in a confirmed, state. The promises of final salvation to Christians are all conditional, either expressly or implied. Perseverance in faith and obedience is the indispensable condition of their salvation.[1]

To change metaphors, you might say that, according to these preachers, getting "saved" is like getting out of prison. Once you're saved, your probation starts. But there's no guarantee you won't violate your probation. If you do, back to prison you go (i.e., to hell).

According to the probation gospel, you aren't guaranteed to go to heaven. If you want to make it there, you need to persevere "in faith and obedience," otherwise you lose what you have.

Do you see why that reasoning would rob someone of assurance?

Assurance of salvation is believe that you have eternal life, that when you die, you'll be with God forever. It knows the moment you believe in Jesus for eternal life you have it as a present possession, and you'll never perish, just as Jesus promised.

Can you have that kind of assurance according to probation salvation?

Nope. And for a very simple, common-sense reason: *you can't see into the future.* Hence, you can't be sure of your salvation, because you can't be sure you'll persevere in faith and obedience to the end of your life.

Do you know what you'll do or believe tomorrow or next week, let alone twelve years from now?

Are you even sure that you'll persist in obedience to Christ by the end of *today*?

Of course, you can't be sure. Hence, you obviously don't have assurance.

Did Jesus Promise Eternal Security?

The best antidote to this problem is to study Jesus' promise, and be absolutely convinced that Jesus preached eternal security, not probation salvation.

Here's one of Jesus' most famous promises:

> "For God loved the world in this way: He gave His One and Only Son, so that everyone who believes in Him will not perish but have eternal life" (John 3:16, HCSB).

Think of this promise in terms of a condition, a consequence, and a guarantee.

First, the *condition* is *faith*. You must believe. Notice the condition is not that you must keep on believing. Salvation requires an act of faith, not a lifetime of faith. That is a major trap some people fall into. They change the condition of salvation from being an act of faith, to being a lifetime of faithfulness.

Consider Abraham. When God told him to

count the stars, and promised Abraham he'd have that many descendants, Abraham believed God's promise, and it was counted as righteousness (Genesis 15:6; Romans 4:3). Abraham's faith was counted as righteousness in that moment, the very second he believed God's promise, not gradually, over a lifetime.

It's the same with *your* justification. The moment you believe the promise, you are justified. The moment you believe in Jesus, something happens, which brings me to the consequence. Your justification before God happens in a single act of faith, not over a lifetime of believing.

Second, the *consequence* is that *believers have eternal life.*

Jesus is promising you that the moment you believe in Him you have eternal life *as a present possession*. It is not something you must earn, keep, or hold on to for dear life the rest of your life. *It is already yours.*

The money was already transferred.

The deed was already signed over.

The bill was already paid.

It's a done deal.

Third, the *guarantee* is *eternal security.* Jesus promises that believers *will not perish*. He doesn't say, you *might* not perish, or that He *hopes* you won't perish, or that you won't perish so long as you're on *your best behavior.*

It's a flat out, unconditional promise.

If you believe, you have eternal life, and will

not perish. Period.

There's no way you can lose your eternal life. Do you believe that?

Here is another promise in which Jesus made the same point:

> "I assure you: Anyone who hears My word and believes Him who sent Me has eternal life and will not come under judgment but has passed from death to life" (John 5:24, HCSB).

Once again, there is a condition, a consequence, and a guarantee.

You already know what the condition and consequence are. If you believe (condition), you have eternal life (consequence). But take a look at the guarantee.

There are three things that Jesus guarantees.

First, believers *have eternal life.* They do not get it in the future. They have it now.

Second, believers *will not come into judgment.* Jesus is referring to what some call the Great White Throne judgment, where the eternal destiny of many is decided at the end of time. Jesus is saying, if you believe, you already have eternal life as a present possession, hence, you will not be judged. That's no longer in your future because it's already happened. You don't have to worry about the Last Judgment, because your fate has already been decided—believers already have eternal life as a present possession. There is no suggestion here that believers can change their status, day-in, and day-out, between being under judgment and not being under judgment.

Third, believers *have passed from death to life.* The moment you believe, you are regenerated and destined to be resurrected in the Messianic age, to experience true life. There is no sense here that believers can pass from death to life today, only to pass back into death next Tuesday, then go back to life again on Sunday during church.

Passing from eternal death to eternal life is a one-time event. Once you believe your fate is sealed (in a good way). Believers are eternally secure from that second on. Life—not death or judgment—is in your future.

Are you a believer?

Do you believe Jesus' promise?

Let's look at one last promise:

> "I give them eternal life, and they will never perish—ever! No one will snatch them out of My hand. My Father, who has given them to Me, is greater than all. No one is able to snatch them out of the Father's hand" (John 10:28-29, HCSB).

I love the emphasis the HCSB puts on Jesus' promise. "They will never perish—*ever!*" Why not?

How can Jesus be so sure?

What is the basis of Jesus' guarantee?

Simple.

Jesus knows that believers will never perish because no one can snatch them out of His, or the Father's, hand. It's like a fireman rescuing a kid from a burning building. "I've got you, kid." Once Jesus and the Father have you in their hands, you're safe and secure from then on, no matter what you do.

In response to this, I have heard some people say, "No one can snatch you out, but you can jump out yourself!"

No, no, no. You can't jump out!

Jesus says *no one* can snatch you out of the Father's hand because the Father is greater than all. "No one" includes *you*. "All" includes *you*.

You don't think God knows we're our own worst enemies? You don't think He knows how badly we mess up our own lives?

You can't jump out of Jesus' hands.

You can't jump out of the Father's hands.

They've got you, and They aren't letting go.

Once you believe, you're safe, you're secure, and no one can snatch you away.

No one.

Not even *you.*

Pardon, Not Probation

If you don't have assurance of salvation because you believe in probation salvation, I hope you'll take Jesus' promise of eternal security seriously. He promised that believers will *never* perish, will not come into judgment, have passed from death to life, and no one, absolutely no one, can snatch them out of His or the Father's hands. It doesn't get clearer than that.

Jesus didn't preach probation. He preached pardon. Full, complete, and irrevocable pardon. All you need do is believe in Him for it.

Do you?

Endnotes

1. J. J. Butler and Ransom Dunn, *Lectures in Systematic Theology* (Boston, MA: The Morning Star Publishing House, 1892), 269, 330-31.

CHAPTER 5

Feelings Over Facts:
The Error of Emotionalism

"TELL ME," the Sunday school teacher began. "How does the story of Lazarus *make you feel*?"

Have you ever noticed that education has come to emphasize feelings over facts? Emotions over arguments? Perceptions over proofs?

Teachers used to ask, "What do you *think* about this?" Now they ask, "What do you *feel* about it?"

It reminds me of a saying here in Texas—"If you don't like the weather, just wait five minutes."

Well, that's what feelings are like—always changing.

Sometimes they're as pleasant as an autumn picnic and other times they come flooding over the levees.

Emotions have their seasons and their cycles and the only constant thing about them is that they're constantly changing.

The emphasis on feelings over facts has been devastating to assurance. Instead of "believing" they're saved, people have sought to "feel" like they're saved. But if your feelings are constantly fluctuating, how can your assurance be anything but fleeting?

Is that *your* struggle?

Have you sought to feel a certain way about being saved? Is that what you think assurance is? Is that what you think assurance is based on?

If so, I want you to consider the case of Martha and Lazarus.

Sad, but Assured

One day Lazarus was sick. Really sick. On the verge of death. And his sisters—Mary and Martha—sent for Jesus, urging Him to come and heal their brother.

But Jesus didn't come.

At least, not right away.

The Lord waited a while, and in the meantime, Lazarus died.

Can you imagine how Martha must have felt?

Grieving for her brother. Disappointed that Jesus didn't respond right away. Bewildered over why God didn't save Lazarus.

Emotionally, she must have been devastated.

Four days later, when Jesus arrived in town, Lazarus was putrefying in the grave. And yet, Martha ran up to Jesus and said,

> "Lord, if You had been here, my brother would not have died. But even now I know that whatever You ask of God, God will give You" (John 11:21b-22).

What amazing faith!

Even though Martha knew full well her brother was as dead as a dog, she believed he could still be brought back to life through Jesus' prayer.

And how did Jesus respond to her confidence in Him? He looked her in the eyes and asked the most critical question of her life,

> "I am the resurrection and the life. He who believes in Me, though he may die, he shall live. And whoever lives and believes in Me shall never die. *Do you believe this?*" (John 11:25-26, emphasis added).

It's one thing to believe God will answer Jesus' prayer to resurrect the dead. It's quite another thing to believe that Jesus Himself *is* the resurrection.

Just because you believe one, doesn't mean you believe the other.

Please notice that Jesus didn't ask Martha how she *felt* about His claims. After all, she just lost her brother, his body was rotting in the tomb, and she was mourning. *Of course, she felt terrible.*

That wasn't Jesus' question.

His question was *did she believe what He said about Himself?*

Did she believe He was the resurrection?

Did she believe He was the life?

Did she believe that Jesus had power over death, and would raise the believing dead back to life in the last day, never to die again?

Well...did she?

> She said to Him, "Yes, Lord, I believe that You are the Christ, the Son of God, who is to come into the world" (John 11:27).

Martha said, "Yes"!

Whatever she *felt* at that moment, she *believed* what Jesus said was true. She believed Jesus could raise up Lazarus. And she believed that *she* would be raised on the Last Day.

Her *heart* may have been full of *sorrow* because of her brother, but her *mind* was full of *faith*, and she had assurance of salvation.

Doubt Your Feelings

How about you? Do you believe what Jesus said about Himself?

Do you have faith, not in God in general, but in Jesus' promise to give resurrection life to believers? Do you believe you will never die, i.e., that you have everlasting life, because you believe in Him?

In short, do you believe that Jesus is the Christ?

If so, you have saving faith. You have assurance.

No matter how you feel about it. No matter how happy or sad you may be right now. No matter how much of a roller coaster the last year has been. No matter how great the coming year might be. Whatever you're feeling should not affect your assurance because assurance comes from believing Jesus' promise, not from your feelings.

Just look at Martha. She was mourning, but she had assurance. The two are not incompatible.

No matter what you're feeling today, you, too, can have assurance, *if* you believe Jesus' promise is true *for you.*

If you've tried to base your assurance on how you feel, you'll be anxious instead of assured. You might have good days and you'll have lots of bad days, but whatever you have, it's not the assurance God wants for you.

God wants you to believe His Son, *no matter how you may be feeling.*

So if you're not sure you're saved, maybe you should doubt your feelings instead of Jesus' promise.

If the Bible says it, don't let your feelings unsettle it.

CHAPTER 6

You Can't Know for Sure: The Error of Skepticism

"HOW CAN YOU know if you believe *any-thing*?"

Daniel was a Reformed Presbyterian pastor. He didn't know if he was truly saved. He knew the *elect* would be, but didn't know if he was among them. He *hoped* he was, of course, but he wasn't *sure*. He had doubts about his salvation and thought *I* should too!

As our discussion progressed, a basic problem revealed itself. Not only did Daniel lack assurance of salvation, he actually wasn't sure *of anything*!

"I mean, I believe a lot of things that I'm not always certain about," he admitted. "I believe Obama is our President. But if I consider the epistemological ramifications of that belief, I may wonder at times if it is really true. I don't know in any strict sense that Obama is President. Perhaps it's really Janet Yellen? In any case, I'm not always confident that what I believe is true."

If you aren't sure who's President, then it's no wonder that you lack assurance!

Daniel was very interested in epistemology, the philosophy of knowledge. Epistemology tries to answer the question, "How do we know anything?"

Sadly, philosophers have always come up short of offering assurance. What I mean is, they have debated these questions for thousands of years, without coming to a solution *that convinces everyone.*

Daniel's particular philosophical tradition denied you could know anything for certain about the world without having special revelation about it (e.g., such as being written in the Bible).

"I *think* I'm married," he told me. "But I don't *know* it. The Bible doesn't say it. So it's only an *opinion* that I have. And, actually, I don't even know if I have that opinion. It's only my opinion that I have that opinion."

The Assurance Syllogism

To see why this led Daniel to doubt his salvation, think of assurance in terms of a very simple syllogism with two premises (P1 and P2) and a conclusion (C). Here it is:

> P1: Jesus promises eternal life to believers.
> P2: I believe.
> C: Therefore I have eternal life.

If you believe P1 and P2, then you must also believe C, that you have eternal life. And if you believe you have eternal life, you have assurance, because that's what assurance is—believing you have eternal life. If you don't believe you have eternal life, well, you don't have assurance!

Simple, right?

Daniel believed P1 because it was in the Scriptures. But he couldn't believe P2 because the Scriptures do not say, "Daniel believed in Jesus." And since he couldn't believe P2, he could not conclude he had everlasting life. Hence, he lacked assurance.

"The only way I could know if I believe is if Scripture had my name written in it and it said, 'Daniel believed.' Since it doesn't say that, I can't know it. And you can't know either, because your name isn't in there!"

Is that the kind of doubt you struggle with?

Do you think you can know whether or not you believe? Is that holding you back from having assurance?

The Bible Assumes You Can Believe

"See to it that no one takes you captive through philosophy and empty deception," Paul warned (Colossians 2:8, NASB).

That warning still applies today. In fact, it may be even more relevant because our culture is steeped in skepticism and relativism, especially when it comes to spiritual things. People are trapped in philosophical positions, without realizing it.

And as Daniel demonstrated, even Christians can fall prey to bad philosophy, even though it claims to be a Christian philosophy!

Daniel wanted to magnify the Word of God, but what actually happened is that he nullified it in his life. The Word of God called him to believe, but his philosophy prevented him from doing it!

For example, take the evangelistic purpose of John's Gospel.

John is revered as the Gospel that most emphasizes faith. In fact, John's Gospel emphasizes faith in Jesus even more than Paul does! In John 20:31, he explained that he wrote his Gospel so his readers would come to faith in Jesus:

> But these are written that *you* may believe that Jesus is the Christ, the Son of God, and that believing *you* may have life in His name (John 20:31, emphasis added).

Notice the *you*. The Gospel was written so that

you may believe and so that *you* may have life in His name.

I'm not the smartest guy in the world, but it seems to me that John expected readers like you to know whether or not you believe in Jesus.

That assumption runs through John.

When Jesus told Martha about the promise of eternal life, He asked her, "Do you believe this?" (John 11:26). In other words, Jesus assumed Martha knew whether or not she believed in Him.

Then Martha answered His question in the affirmative. "Yes, Lord; I believe," she said (John 11:27). Martha knew whether or not she believed.

So the Bible assumes you can know if you believe. Whatever doubts have been created by your philosophy, I urge you to put them to one side, and yield to the Bible's common sense. Don't let bad philosophy get in the way of the Word of God's clear address to you. Let John's purpose statement cut through the confusion created by skepticism.

Jesus' question to Martha in John 11:26 is John's own implied question to you—do you believe in Jesus for everlasting life?

In that case, what do you have, right now?

CHAPTER 7

Did Jesus Die for Me?
The Error of Limited Atonement

"HOW DO YOU know Jesus died for you? What makes you so special?"

I was talking to a Presbyterian named Craig who lacked assurance. I told him I had assurance of salvation. I knew Jesus died for me on the cross, and offered me everlasting life through faith in Him. And since I believed His promise, I knew I had everlasting life.

But Craig had doubts.

"Don't you believe Jesus died for you?" I asked.

"I don't know. I hope so, but I don't know for sure," he admitted.

"When you evangelize, don't you tell people that Jesus died for them?"

"No! I don't urge people to believe that because that might not be true."

Oh, boy.

If you're not a Calvinist, you might not understand what Craig meant.

You see, according to Calvinist theology, God doesn't love everyone and Jesus didn't die for everyone. Instead, Calvinists believe God created some people for salvation and others to damnation, punished forever for sins He predestined them to commit. And so, in their view, God sent Jesus to die for the elect only, and gives the gift of saving faith to the elect only. Everyone else is doomed to hell. And that brings God glory.

This creates an awful problem for Calvinists seeking assurance. They can never figure out which group they're in. Are they one of the people Jesus died for, or one of the ones Jesus passed over?

Is that your struggle?

Do you doubt that God loves you and that Jesus died for you? If so, no wonder you lack assurance.

If your church or denomination denies that God loves everyone, or denies Jesus died for everyone, I would strongly suggest *running as fast as you can in the other direction.* You don't want to attend a church that doesn't understand something as basic as God's love and the extent of the cross.

Imagine if your church taught wives they could never be certain their husbands loved them, or taught children they can never be sure if their parents were actually out to murder them. Do you think that would be a helpful or harmful message?

Let me be absolutely clear about this   it is diabolically false to deny that God loves everyone or deny that Jesus died for everyone.

He did.

I'll prove it.

God Loves You

God could not have made it any clearer that He loves *the world*. That means everyone, including *you*.

> "For God so *loved the world* that He gave His only begotten Son, that whoever believes in Him should not perish but have everlasting life" (John 3:16, emphasis added).

Are you part of the world? Of course you are. Then God loves you too.

But if you persist in thinking you must be an enemy of God, then let me remind you of how Jesus said we should treat our enemies:

> "But I say to you, *love your enemies*, bless those who curse you, do good to those who hate you, and pray for those who spitefully use you and persecute you" (Matthew 5:44, emphasis added).

"But I say to you who hear: '*Love your
enemies*, do good to those who hate you'"
(Luke 6:27, emphasis added).

"But *love your enemies*, do good, and lend,
hoping for nothing in return; and your
reward will be great, and you will be sons
of the Most High. For He is kind to the
unthankful and evil" (Luke 6:35, emphasis
added).

If God commands us to love our enemies,
wouldn't He do the same? Would He command us
to do something good, that He Himself does not
do?

Are you better than God?

Of course not.

God commanded us to love our enemies
because that's what He does, too. It's part of His
loving character.

Think of it this way. Even if you were convinced that God created you to be His enemy, how
does God want enemies to be treated? With love.

That means even if you were God's enemy, He
would love you.

He would do good to you.

He would bless you.

Yes, He would even die for you.

Even God's enemies are not excluded from His
love.

As John 3:16 says, "God so loved the world,"

no exceptions. Including you.

Jesus Died for You

Since God loves the world, and even has a special and explicit love for enemies, whom do you think Jesus died for?

Here again, God couldn't have made it any clearer. The plain Biblical testimony is that Jesus died for everyone, for all humanity, for the whole world.

> "Here is the Lamb of God, who takes away the sin of the world!" (John 1:29, HCSB).

> "We know that this man really is the Savior of the world" (John 4:42, HCSB).

> And He Himself is the propitiation for our sins; and not for ours only, but also for those of the whole world (1 John 2:2, NASB).

> And we have seen and testify that the Father has sent his Son to be the Savior of the world (1 John 4:14).

Are you getting the impression that Jesus died for the whole world?

Can language be any clearer?

If God wanted you to know that Jesus died for

everyone, what more could He say?

If Jesus even died for false teachers who deny Him (2 Peter 2:1), then He died for you too.

Jesus Promised You

The Bible clearly says that God loves you, and sent Jesus to die for you. But has He promised you everlasting life?

Yes, He has.

When John wrote his Gospel, he had a very specific purpose in mind. He meant it to be evangelistic. He wrote it so that unbelievers would believe in Jesus and have everlasting life.

> "Very truly I tell you, *whoever hears my word* and *believes* him who sent me has eternal life and will not be judged but has crossed over from death to life" (John 5:24, NIV).

Are you a "whoever"? Have you heard the promise? Then I have good news: *the promise applies to you.* Forget about theoretical questions about predestination and election and the extent of the atonement. Just pay attention to the simple meaning of Scripture.

You've heard the promise. It's for you. If you believe it, you have eternal life.

John was very explicit about the evangelistic purpose of his Gospel. Here is how he put it:

But these are written so that *you* may
believe Jesus is the Messiah, the Son of
God, and by believing *you* may have life
in His name (John 20:31, HCSB, emphasis
added).

Are you a "you"? If you are (and what else
would you be?), then according to John 20:31,
you can believe that Jesus is the Messiah, and by
believing, have life in His name.

In other words, the promise of eternal life is
for you. Don't let highly questionable theories of
election and predestination distract you from that
simple truth.[1]

If you lacked assurance because you weren't
sure that God loved you, or that Jesus died for
you, or that He offered you eternal life, then I
hope you realize your picture of God was all
wrong.

God is love (1 John 4:8). If anyone tells you
differently, go back to the Bible, and listen to what
Jesus said about it.

More importantly, *believe* what He said. If you
do believe the promise, you are born again, have
that life as a present possession, and will be with
God forever.

Endnotes

1. I believe most of the literature on predestination and election, while very interesting, and

intellectually stimulating, is mostly mistaken about what the Bible actually says on those topics. It mostly comes from philosophy, not the Bible.

Instead, I believe the Bible presents election as God's (and man's) choices of people, places, and things, *for service,* not *for eternal life.* In other words, so far as I can see, the Bible does not speak about the election of individuals to eternal life (or the equivalent). A couple of verses in Romans and Ephesians come close, but don't hold up under scrutiny. But people, places, and things are chosen to serve God's purposes in some way: as the chosen city, the chosen Temple, as priests, kings, and apostles. And above all, as Savior of the world.

For more information, see Robert N. Wilkin, "The Doctrine Of Divine Election Reconsidered: Election To Service, Not To Everlasting Life," *Journal of the Grace Evangelical Society* (Autumn 2012): 3-22; Shawn C. Lazar, *Chosen to Serve: A Vocational View of Election* (Denton, TX: Grace Evangelical Society, 2017, forthcoming).

CHAPTER 8

Dead Faith: The Error of Reading James Evangelistically

"SURE, SURE, WE both agree we're saved by faith apart from works," the pastor assured me. "But obviously, faith without works *is dead*."

He was quoting James 2:17.

If you teach salvation by faith apart from works, someone will eventually quote from James, which is often interpreted to teach that you only gain eternal salvation by faith that works.

Consequently, I have met countless people who aren't sure of their salvation because while they say they believe, they aren't sure if they have the right kind of faith—whether their faith is alive or dead.

Do you, too, wonder about that?

Are you doubting your salvation because you

aren't sure if you have the right kind of faith?

If so, the best solution is to get a better grasp of what James actually meant.

Biblical Wisdom

People often read James as if it were an evangelistic tract concerned with telling you the condition for *eternal salvation*, when it is really Wisdom Literature concerned with telling you the conditions for *earthly salvation*.

In other words, they read James alongside John's Gospel or Paul's letters to the Galatians and the Romans, when they should be reading it alongside Proverbs, Ecclesiastes, or the Sermon on the Mount.

You might say that most people are forcing James to sing in the wrong key—they've got him singing about how to get to heaven, when he's really singing about how to live on earth.

The Epistle of James is Wisdom Literature. I'm hardly the first person to recognize that.[1] Wisdom books are concerned with earthly salvation. They are not meant to tell you how to be born-again, but how to live well *in this life,* after you are born-again.

How can you prosper?

How can you have a good marriage, a good family life, and live well with others?

How can you avoid suffering the bad consequences of sin?

How can you avoid an early death?

How can you avoid wasting your earthly life?

Those are the concerns of Wisdom Literature, and those are James's concerns as well.

As he tells us in the opening verses, James is concerned that his readers know how to deal with *earthly trials*.

> My brethren, count it all joy when you fall into various trials (James 1:2).

That sets the theme for the rest of the book. James is not writing evangelistically to unbelievers hoping they'll come to faith in Christ for the first time. Rather, he's writing to believers (his "brethren") hoping that earthly trials will help them mature:

> Knowing that the testing of your faith produces patience. But let patience have its perfect work, that you may be perfect and complete, lacking nothing (James 1:3-4).

James wants his believing readers to be complete in their Christian character and to lack nothing in their walk with the Lord on this earth.

And what do we need for that?

Wisdom.

But where does wisdom come from? According to Wisdom Literature, God gives it.

> For the Lord gives wisdom; from His

mouth come knowledge and understanding (Proverbs 2:6).

Likewise, according to James, when you face
the trials of life, you need to ask God for wisdom:

> If any of you lacks wisdom, let him ask of
> God, who gives to all liberally and with-
> out reproach, and it will be given to him
> (James 1:5).

When you read James alongside other Wisdom books, you can't help but see the many paral-
lels. Both are concerned with wisdom for practical
living.

Sin Is Deadly

One of the major concerns of Wisdom Literature is with the deadly consequences of sin.

To be clear, by "deadly" I mean *physical death*
in the here and now, not *eternal death* in the hereafter.

And according to Wisdom books, it is prover-
bially true that while a godly life will be long and
prosperous, an ungodly life will result in an early
death. In other words, sin can literally get you
killed.

For example, I remember my wife and I lived
in a bad neighborhood in Baton Rouge, where
hearing gunfire outside our window was a regular
occurrence. When we asked our landlady about it,

she said, "That's just the drug dealers killing each other. You've nothing to worry about." We moved to Texas shortly after!

Those dead drug dealers, most of whom were young men, illustrate that sin can have deadly consequences in this life. Just open up any newspaper and you'll read about angry husbands killing their cheating wives, celebrities dying of drug overdoses, thieves getting shot by store clerks, gang violence, abortion, and suicide bombings.

And that isn't counting all the private mental sins that eat us up inside, affecting our mental health, emotional health, and even physical health. "When I kept silent about my sin, my body wasted away," David warned (Psalm 32:3a, NASB).

Who can doubt that sin is deadly?

Hence, Wisdom Literature is meant to lead the wise away from the deadly consequences of sin, so they can enjoy a full and satisfying life here on earth, as God intended.

For example, here is what Proverbs has to say:

> My son, don't forget my teaching, but let your heart keep my commands; for they will bring you many days, a full life, and well-being (Proverbs 3:1-2, HCSB).

> Listen, my son. Accept my words, and you will live many years (Proverbs 4:10, HCSB).

> For through wisdom your days will be
> many, and years will be added to your life
> (Proverbs 9:11, NIV).

By contrast, if you ignore wisdom and live in sin, you will suffer its deadly consequences:

> The fear of the Lord prolongs days, but
> the years of the wicked will be shortened
> (Proverbs 10:27).

> As righteousness leads to life, so he who
> pursues evil pursues it to his own death
> (Proverbs 11:19).

> There is life in the path of righteousness,
> but another path leads to death (Proverbs
> 12:28, HCSB).

Likewise, James is also concerned about living wisely to avoid an early death:

> But each one is tempted when he is drawn
> away by his own desires and enticed.
> Then, when desire has conceived, it gives
> birth to sin; and sin, when it is full-grown,
> *brings forth death* (James 1:14-15, empha-
> sis added).

In fact, Proverbs says that a wise man will turn others from their sins so they can avoid an early physical death:

> A wise man's instruction is a fountain of life, turning people away from the snares of death (Proverbs 13:14, HCSB).

It should come as no surprise that James has the same concern. Believers should turn others from their sins, so they won't die:

> Let him know that he who turns a sinner from the error of his way will save his soul from death and will cover a multitude of sins (James 5:20, NASB).

James is Wisdom Literature. It deals with *earthly salvation*, not with *eternal salvation*. The epistle's focus is on teaching believers to put their faith into practice, and not on explaining to unbelievers the conditions for having eternal life.

Shared Themes

There are many shared themes between James and other Wisdom books. Here are just a few more examples to convince you that James should not be read as an evangelistic tract, but as a book concerned with practical living.

For example, both James and Wisdom Literature are concerned about employers paying fair wages to laborers:

> "You shall not cheat your neighbor, nor rob him. The wages of him who is hired shall not remain with you all night until morning" (Leviticus 19:13).

> Look! The wages you failed to pay the workers who mowed your fields are crying out against you. The cries of the harvesters have reached the ears of the Lord Almighty (James 5:4, NIV).

I've read many evangelistic tracts, and none of them have ever mentioned paying workers in a timely manner. But that is exactly the kind of thing that Wisdom Literature is concerned about.

Both James and Wisdom Literature advise thinking before you speak:

> The mind of the righteous person thinks before answering, but the mouth of the wicked blurts out evil things (Proverbs 15:28, HCSB).

> But everyone must be quick to hear, slow to speak and slow to anger (James 1:19b, NASB).

In fact, there is a great emphasis on controlling our tongues in general:

Whoever guards his mouth and tongue
keeps his soul from troubles (Proverbs
21:23; cf. 10:19; 12:13).

And the tongue is a fire, a world of iniqui-
ty. The tongue is so set among our mem-
bers that it defiles the whole body, and sets
on fire the course of nature; and it is set on
fire by hell (James 3:6).

Both James and Wisdom Literature have an
obvious concern for helping the poor:

She extends her hand to the poor, yes, she
reaches out her hands to the needy (Proverbs 31:20).

If a brother or sister is naked and desti-
tute of daily food, and one of you says to
them, "Depart in peace, be warmed and
filled," but you do not give them the things
which are needed for the body, what does
it profit? (James 2:15 16).

And they both warn against speaking evil of
our neighbors:

He who is devoid of wisdom despises his
neighbor; but a man of understanding
holds his peace (Proverbs 11:12).

Do not speak evil of one another, brethren. He who speaks evil of a brother and judges his brother, speaks evil of the law and judges the law. But if you judge the law, you are not a doer of the law but a judge (James 4:11).

Confessing your sins to one another is also important:

He who covers his sins will not prosper, but whoever confesses and forsakes them will have mercy (Proverbs 28:13).

Confess your trespasses to one another, and pray for one another, that you may be healed. The effective, fervent prayer of a righteous man avails much (James 5:16).

Do I need to go on? Is it clear to you that James is Wisdom Literature?

None of these themes make sense if James were an evangelistic tract telling unbelievers the condition of eternal salvation. But they make perfect sense if he was instructing believers how to live wisely.

As I mentioned above, I'm not the first person to recognize that James is Christian Wisdom Literature. In fact, I would say that is the near consensus among scholars, across denominational lines. But unlike many, I have tried to take that insight very seriously, by trying to re-read the famous problem passages about faith and works in light of the Wisdom tradition. Typically, those passages have been read as if they were evangelistic statements. But if James is Wisdom Literature, how does that change their meaning?

Dead Faith?

> Even so faith, if it has no works, is dead, being by itself (James 2:17, NASB).

When some interpreters read James as an evangelistic tract, they think James 2:17 means that if you don't have works, *you don't really believe*, and if you don't really believe, you'll go to hell.

The problem is, that interpretation clearly contradicts Paul's and John's emphasis that the *only* condition of salvation is to *believe in Jesus*—works are excluded as a condition of eternal salvation (e.g., John 3:15-16, 36; 5:24; 6:29; Galatians 2:16; Romans 3:20; Ephesians 2:8-9).

But when you approach James as Wisdom Literature—concerned with earthly salvation—this verse makes perfect sense, and doesn't contradict Paul and John at all.

When James talks about "dead faith," he isn't talking about a faith that *doesn't really exist*. He's saying the faith without works is *useless* when confronting the trials of life. "It's as useless as a dead dog," as we say in Texas (cf. 2 Samuel 16:9,

CEV). In fact, that's how James 2:20 puts it, "But are you willing to recognize, you foolish fellow, that faith without works is useless?"

It is easy to see why this would be of concern for Wisdom Literature.

For example, faith without works is useless for helping people who are "without clothing and in need of daily food" (James 2:15, NASB). If you want to deliver someone from hunger, you need to do more than believe—you must put your faith into action and actually feed him!

Faith alone doesn't make a sandwich for the hungry.

Faith alone doesn't change diapers on a crying baby.

Faith alone doesn't help a friend fill out job applications.

Faith alone doesn't pay the bills, comfort those in mourning, or lend a helping hand when a friend moves.

If you want to face those practical problems—James's trials of life—you need more than faith alone, but faith that works. As James says elsewhere,

> But prove yourselves doers of the word,
> and not merely hearers who delude them-
> selves (James 1:22, NASB).

Just do it. You might say that's what Wisdom Literature is all about.

Can Faith Save Him?

The second problem passage builds on the first.

> What does it profit, my brethren, if someone says he has faith but does not have works? Can faith save him? (James 2:14).

This is a rhetorical question. James expects the answer to be, "No, it can't save him." The big question here is, save him from what? What kind of salvation is in view here?

If you read James as an evangelistic tract, you'll think, "Save him *from hell*." Hence, you'll think that James is teaching that faith without works cannot give you *eternal salvation*. However, that interpretation has absolutely nothing to do with the context of the passage or with the overall message of the epistle.

But when you keep Wisdom Literature in mind, James's meaning is obvious. The "profit" he is talking about is living well now, as a spiritually mature person. The salvation he is concerned about is with *earthly salvation*. Can faith without works save you from the deadly consequences of sin? Can it save your from the trials of life? Faith without works is useless. If you say you have faith, but don't act on it, you won't be saved from earthly trials and the deadly consequences of sin. In fact, if you act *against* your faith, and live foolishly and sinfully, you might die an early death.

Demonic Faith

The third passage mentions that the demons are monotheists. For some reason, people who object to the faith-alone message use this passage to show that mere "intellectual faith" in Jesus is not enough to be saved. You need "heart faith," they say, something the demons do not have.

It's a neat idea, but those ideas are literally not mentioned in the text. It's not at all what James was discussing. James wrote,

> You believe that there is one God. You do well. Even the demons believe—and tremble! (James 2:19).

This has nothing to do with intellectual faith vs heart faith. James is saying that while the demons are monotheists (i.e., they believe in one God), they haven't put even that limited faith into practice. Instead, they rebel against God. So their faith is useless.

By contrast, as James goes on to explain, Abraham did put his faith into practice when he obeyed God by agreeing to sacrifice his promised son, Isaac. Abraham had not always consistently obeyed God earlier in his life, but by obeying God's command to sacrifice Isaac, Abraham proved that his faith was mature; he was vindicated:

> Was not Abraham our father justified by

works when he offered Isaac his son on
the altar? Do you see that faith was working together with his works, and by works
faith was made perfect? And the Scripture
was fulfilled which says, "Abraham believed God, and it was accounted to him
for righteousness." And he was called the
friend of God. You see then that a man is
justified by works, and not by faith only
(James 2:21-24).

People who read James as an evangelistic tract
immediately think that he is talking about the
Pauline sense of justification, i.e., being forensi-
cally reckoned as righteous before God. But justification is also an important concept in Wisdom
Literature, albeit with a different meaning. We see
that in Jesus' own teaching:

"Wisdom is justified by her children"
(Matthew 11:19; Luke 7:35).

What kind of justification is this? Not the Pauline kind. Wisdom is not justified by her children
in the sense of having righteousness imputed to
her by faith in Christ. In Wisdom Literature, to be
justified simply means *to be proved right*. Wisdom
is proved right by the good consequences that
follow from acting wisely. That's the kind of justification that James is talking about in reference
to Abraham—not forensic righteousness before
God, but vindication before men. As Phil Stringer

explained,

> We are justified before men by our works
> (Ephesians 2:10; Titus 2:11-13). This is our
> testimony. We are justified by faith before
> God—this is our salvation (Romans 4:1-
> 8).[2]

Or as Paul said,

> If Abraham was justified by works, he has
> something to boast about, *but not before*
> *God* (Romans 4:2, emphasis added).

Paul admitted there was a justification by
works, *but not before God.* Then before whom?
Obviously, before *other people.*

Abraham's willingness to sacrifice his long-
awaited, promised son, showed other people—including you and me—that he knew and believed
God. In particular, Abraham was willing to sacrifice Isaac because he believed God could raise him
from the dead (Hebrews 11:19). We can see the
good consequences of his faith, and recognize that
Abraham's faith in God was justified.

Conclusion

Is faith without works dead? Yes. It will be useless to you when you face the trials of life.

Can faith without works save you from earthly

trials and dangers? No. If you want to grow and prosper and mature in your faith, you need to put God's Word into practice.

Does that mean we are eternally saved by a mixture of faith and works? No, because James is not teaching about eternal salvation, but earthly salvation.

Does that mean we should redefine faith to include works? No again. Faith is one thing and works are another.

Have you been worried about your eternal salvation because you aren't sure if your faith is alive, or dead?

Well, now you know that James was talking about earthly salvation. I think an argument can be made that while you can be sure of your eternal salvation, you can't be sure of your earthly salvation.

Why not?

Because earthly salvation all depends on you. It all depends on how you're putting your faith into practice. And since your behavior isn't always consistent, and you have no idea how you'll act in the future, you'll probably lack assurance of earthly salvation. Not always, but sometimes.

By contrast, assurance of eternal salvation is not based on what you do, but based on simply believing Jesus' promise of eternal life (John 3:16). You can be sure of that salvation because it isn't based on what you've done, but on what Jesus has promised to do for believers.

It would be wise to believe Him.[3]

Endnotes

1. For example, here is a quote from some Catholic Bishops: "From the viewpoint of its literary form, James is a letter only in the most conventional sense; it has none of the characteristic features of a real letter except the address. It belongs rather to the genre of parenesis or exhortation and is concerned almost exclusively with ethical conduct. It therefore falls within the tradition of Jewish wisdom literature, such as can be found in the Old Testament (Proverbs, Sirach) and in the extracanonical Jewish literature (Testaments of the Twelve Patriarchs, the Books of Enoch, the Manual of Discipline found at Qumran)." See http://www.usccb.org/bible/james/0. Accessed February 22, 2017. For other examples, see John A. Burns, "James, the Wisdom of Jesus," *Criswell Theological Review* 1.1 (1986) 113-135; Robert F. Chaffin, Jr., "The Theme of Wisdom in the Epistle of James," *Ashland Theological Journal* 29 (1997): 23-49; Gary Holloway, "James as New Testament Wisdom Literature," *Leaven*, Vol. 8 [2000], Iss. 2: 89-95.

2. Jim Scudder and Phil Stringer, *Evangelism Made Simple: How a Clear Presentation of the Gospel Can make Your Witnessing More Effective*

(Lake Zurich, IL: Victory In Grace, 2016), 93.

3. Two commentaries that are very helpful for understanding James's concern with earthly salvation are, Zane C. Hodges, *The Epistle of James: Proven Character Through Testing* (Denton, TX: Grace Evangelical Society, 2009, 2016); and John F. Hart, "James," in *The Moody Bible Commentary*, eds. Michael A Rydelnik and Michael Vanlaningham (Chicago, IL: Moody, 2014).

CHAPTER 9

Is Doubt Humble?
The Error of Uncertainty

IS IT JUST me, or do people seem proud of their doubts about Jesus? It's considered a sign of humility, and the only reasonable stance towards religious claims. As noted TV personality and "apatheist" (i.e., apathetic atheist), Bill Maher said,

> "The only appropriate attitude for man to have about the big questions is not the arrogant certitude that is the hallmark of religion, but doubt. Doubt is humble."[1]

Many Christians feel the same way, even pastors! They teach it's normal to constantly doubt God and His Word.

"Faith is like yogurt," one pastor explained.

"Doubts are the berries on top. They need to be mixed in with the yogurt. If you were missing the berries in your meal, your faith would be incomplete. You could still eat it, but it would miss the flavor it was meant to have."[2]

Or here's Philip Yancey, "Where there is certainty there is no room for faith."[3]

Is that true?

Is faith meant to be mixed with doubt? Was that really God's plan?

Are you supposed to doubt that Jesus died on the cross, that He was the propitiation for your sin, that He loves you, and that He wants you to believe in Him for everlasting life? That God doesn't want you to be sure of any of those things?

Is that what you believe?

Are you *sure* about that?

If you think that assurance is arrogant, and doubting Jesus is a sign of healthy humility, then the reason why you lack assurance may be because *you don't actually want it*!

If that describes you, then I want to show you that doubt, far from being God's will for you, is a debilitating sin.

Adam and Eve

Think back to Adam and Eve. Why did they go wrong? We all know they ate the forbidden fruit and humanity fell. But what led to that fateful decision?

It all began with doubt.

When God created Adam and Eve, He abundantly provided for all their needs. They could reach out and grab whatever food they wanted. They had everything they needed

But God had one, simple, modest, rule:

> "You are free to eat from any tree of the garden, but you must not eat from the tree of the knowledge of good and evil, for on the day you eat from it, you will certainly die" (Genesis 2:16-17, HCSB).

God's command was as clear as the noonday sun. "See that fruit over there? On that tree? You see it? *Don't eat it.*"

They could even eat from the tree of life (Genesis 2:9)!

In other words, God wasn't holding any good thing back from them. They just had to stay away from that one tree.

Just one.

What could be simpler?

And yet the serpent managed to deceive them. But how?

It all started with doubt.

Seeds of Doubt

The Serpent approached Eve and asked, "Did

God really say, 'You can't eat from *any tree* in the garden'?" (Genesis 3:1, HCSB, emphasis added).

Notice what the serpent did there.

He tried to plant seeds of doubt in Eve's mind. "Did God really say...?" The serpent wanted Eve to question God's command. And to do that, the serpent deliberately misquoted God. God didn't say, "You can't eat from *any* tree." He said, "Don't eat from *that* tree."

So Eve corrected the serpent. "We may eat the fruit from the trees in the garden. But about the fruit of the tree in the middle of the garden, God said, 'You must not eat it or touch it, or you will die" (Genesis 3:2, HCSB).

Then the serpent tried a different tactic. He directly contradicted God's Word. "No! You will not die," he brazenly lied (Genesis 3:4, HCSB). He went on to call God's character into question. "In fact, God knows that when you eat it your eyes will be opened and you will be like God, knowing good and evil" (Genesis 3:4-5, HCSB).

The serpent wanted Eve to believe that God was selfishly keeping back something good from her.

And how did Eve respond?

She looked at the fruit, saw it was good to eat, believed the serpent and took a bite.

Doubt won.

How Did the Serpent Win?

How did the serpent get Adam and Eve to disobey God?

He couldn't *force* them to. Sin is a moral action, a choice of the will to disobey God's Law. It begins in the heart (Genesis 6:5; Proverbs 6:18; Matthew 15:19; Romans 1:28). Moral actions require free choices. If, say, the serpent had physically forced Eve to pick, chew, and swallow the fruit, she would not have sinned, because it was not her action.

The serpent did not have the power to *cause* Eve to do anything. He only had the power to *influence* her. Satan can try to sell you his wares, but he can't force you to buy. That's your choice. All Satan can do is influence you to choose his way. And the way to influence a moral being *is through his mind.*

While God sought to influence Eve by presenting His goodness, kindness, and truth, Satan sought to influence her through misdirection, deception, and doubt.

Two different influences.

Two different paths.

God's command implies a choice: you can either obey or disobey. If you didn't have a choice, the command would be pointless. And if the choice was actually God's to make—not Eve's, and not yours—then God would be responsible for all the evil in the world, which is blasphemous.

Eve was free to choose whether to obey or disobey. Sadly, she chose wrongly.

Doubt led to her devastation.

I don't understand why some Evangelicals consider doubting God a virtue, or why they make it an aspect of humility. As Martin Luther reminds us,

> What else are we doing by our unbelief or doubt than charging God with a lie when He gives His promise and confirms it with an oath? We are defying Him to His face, as it were, and we are saying: Lord God, You are lying.[4]

Doubt is a vice. It makes God out to be a liar—or at least, considers the *possibility* that He might be a liar.

Doubting God isn't humble, but prideful. It means disagreeing with God. The Lord tells you something and you disagree, so you doubt Him. That isn't humility, but very same kind of pride that led to the Fall.

God does not want you to doubt.

"O you of little faith, why did you doubt?" Jesus once asked Peter (Matthew 14:31).

Or, as James taught us about prayer, "let him ask in faith, with no doubting, for he who doubts is like a wave of the sea driven and tossed by the wind" (James 1:6).

Does it seem to you that Jesus and James had a

positive view of doubt?

Obviously not.

Don't Doubt Jesus

Don't get me wrong. I encourage you to be inquisitive. I encourage you to seek the truth wherever it may be found. I encourage you to ask questions, to think deeply, and to reconsider previously held beliefs in order to develop a self-conscious, and deeply rooted faith. That's what I'm asking you to do in this book.

However, don't get *comfortable* with doubt.

Don't think it's *normal*.

Don't think God *wants* you to doubt Him, as if that somehow pleases Him, or makes life better.

Would you want your kids or spouse to always doubt that you loved them? Would you want your employer to doubt everything you did and said? Would you want your friends to never be sure if they could believe you?

Of course not.

Doubt happens. But that's not the same as saying it's God's will for you.

In fact, instead of becoming comfortable with doubt, realize it often leads you to become estranged from God, just as it did with Adam and Eve.

And above all, don't doubt Jesus' promise of everlasting life!

J. Wilbur Chapman told the story of meeting with D. L. Moody in Chicago. "Mr. Moody," he began, "I am not sure whether I am a Christian or not."

Moody turned to John 5:24: "Verily, verily, I say unto you, he that heareth my word, and believeth on Him that sent me, hath everlasting life, and shall not come into condemnation: but is passed from death unto life."

"Do you believe it?" Moody asked.

He said, "Yes."

"Well, are you a Christian?" Moody asked.

"Sometimes I think I am, and sometimes I am afraid I am not."

Moody told him to read the verse again, and said, "Do you believe it?"

"Yes," Chapman said.

"Do you receive Him?"

"Yes."

"Well," he said, "are you a Christian?"

As Chapman was about to express his doubts again, Moody turned on him with his eyes flashing and said, "See here, whom are you doubting?"

Then Chapman saw it. He lacked assurance—not because assurance was something other than faith—but because he was doubting Jesus' promise.[5]

If you lack assurance because you doubt Jesus' promise of eternal life, I would urge you to reconsider Whom you are doubting.

Endnotes

1. http://www.imdb.com/title/tt0815241/quotes

2. Adapted from Luke Larsen, "How Doubt Saved My Faith" *Relevant.* See http://www.relevantmagazine.com/god/how-doubt-saved-my-faith

3. http://philipyancey.com/q-and-a-topics/faith-and-doubt

4. *What Luther Says: A Practical In-Home Anthology for the Active Christian*, ed. Ewald M. Plass (Saint Louis, MO: Concordia Publishing House, 1959), 428.

5. Adapted from J. Wilbur Chapman, "Are You a Christian?" See https://faithalone.org/magazine/y1989/89feb5.html. Accessed January 16, 2017.

Conclusion

HAVE YOU EVER heard the term "easy believism"? Preachers use it to mock the faith alone
message.

On the one hand, I think it's a good label. I
accept it. *I believe in easy believism.* Why? Because
salvation *is* easy...for believers!

The only condition to be saved is to believe in
Jesus for that salvation. You can't work for it, earn
it, or otherwise *behave* yourself into heaven. All
that Jesus requires for salvation is to believe in
Him for it.

Salvation is easy...*for us*. But it wasn't easy for
Jesus! He had to live a sinless life to qualify as the
Lamb of God who takes away the sins of the world
(John 1:29). Then He suffered and died on the
cross to make propitiation for sin, and rose again

from the dead as the first-fruits of our own future resurrection. Salvation was hard for Jesus.

I wonder what the people who deny "easy believism" teach about salvation? Do they teach "hard believism"? "Easy worksism"? "Hard worksism"?

In my experience, people who denounce "easy believism" are usually very confused about the nature of faith and the condition of salvation.

They think faith means all kinds of things—from emotional upheavals, to existential leaps, to mystical experiences. And as a result of that confusion, they often aren't sure if they really have genuine faith themselves!

So they turn to works, and teach that salvation depends, in some sense, on our behavior. Doing good works, they say, either makes faith genuine, or earns salvation, or is necessary to keep our salvation, or at the very least proves that we have salvation. And since they aren't sure if they really believe, or if they'll do enough good works to warrant going to heaven, they lack assurance. And their own doubts spread like fog from the pulpits to the pews.

Maybe you've been lost in that fog.

Maybe you've been unsure about what it means to believe, or you've thought your salvation depended on works in some way.

I hope you see now why that's wrong.

I hope you understand that faith simply means to believe that something is true, and that saving faith means to believe that Jesus' promise of eternal life is true.

And I hope you understand that having assurance of salvation means simply believing, "I have everlasting life," not because you worked for it, but because *that's what Jesus guarantees believers.*

Actually, I hope you do more than merely *understand* all that, but *believe* it too. For when you believe *that*, you cannot help but have assurance of salvation, because that is exactly what Jesus asks you to believe—that believers *have* eternal life.

Appendices

Defining Faith

"WHAT IS *TIME*?" Augustine mused. "If no one asks me, I know what it is. But if I need to explain it to someone, I do not know."

Do you ever feel the same way about *faith*?

Maybe after reading the previous chapters you do.

When you aren't thinking about it, you know what faith is. (Or at least you *think* you do.) But as soon as someone asks you to define it, you get tongue-tied and confused. You might even have to confess you don't know what faith is after all.

But if you don't know what it means to believe, you'll have a serious obstacle towards having assurance.

Think about it.

If you believe that faith is the only condition

of salvation but aren't sure what faith is, then how can you be sure you've met the condition of salvation?

Obviously, you can't. And if you can't be sure you've met the condition of salvation, you can't be sure that you're saved. Hence, you'll lack assurance.

Clearly, if you want assurance, you need to know what it means to believe.

So, what is faith?

Thankfully, the answer is so simple, even a child can understand it.

Dictionary Definitions

Here's how Webster's 1828 dictionary defined the word *believe*:

> BELIEVE, *verb transitive.* To credit upon the authority or testimony of another; *to be persuaded of the truth of something* upon the declaration of another, or upon evidence furnished by reasons, arguments, and deductions of the mind, or by other circumstances, than personal knowledge (emphasis added).[1]

To believe is to be persuaded that some declaration is true.

Simple, right?

If you think something is true, you believe it.

Of course, the real question is not what *believe* means in *English*, but what it means in *Greek*, especially in places like John 3:16, in which Jesus promises, "whosoever believes has eternal life."

The Greek word for *believe* is the verb *pisteuō*. Here is the very first definition given by BDAG, the leading New Testament Greek Lexicon:

> 1. *to consider something to be true* and therefore worthy of one's trust, believe (emphasis added).[2]

Once again, to believe something, is to consider it to be true.

So, in both English and in Greek, the basic meaning of *believe* is to *consider something to be true*. If you consider something to be true, then you believe it.

Imagine if someone told you that cutting sugar out of your diet would improve your health, or that winter in Canada is colder than winter in Southern California, or that grizzly bears are more dangerous than turtles, and you said, "I believe that." What do you mean? Aren't you saying you think those statements are *true*?

Contrariwise, imagine if someone told you that the moon is made out of green cheese, or Mohammed is a prophet of Allah, or the next soft jazz track will be even better than the last one. And you said, "No way, I don't believe that." When you are persuaded that some statement, promise,

or claim is *false*, that means you *don't believe it.*
Simple, right?

Before You Can Believe

When you are persuaded that something is true, two things must happen first.

First, you must *understand* what is being said. Older theologians called this *notitia*, understanding. If you don't understand something, then you can't believe it is either true or false. Think of Nicodemus being told about the new birth in John 3. He didn't even understand what it meant to be born again, so of course he could not believe in Jesus for that.

Second, you must *believe it.* Older theologians called this *assent.* After you understand what it being said (e.g., how to be born again), you can assent to it. In other words, you think it is true.

That's what faith consists of: understanding and assent.

You don't believe everything that you understand. For example, I understand that Mohammed, Joseph Smith, and Pope Francis all claim to speak for God...but I don't believe it.

Abraham Believed God

If you want a paradigmatic example of what it means to believe, consider Abraham.

When God brought him out at night to count the stars, God said to him,

> "Look now toward heaven, and count the stars if you are able to number them." And He said to him, "So shall your descendants be" (Genesis 15:5).

God uttered a statement, namely, a promise. Abraham—who was old and childless at the time—would have as many descendants as the stars. And what did Abraham (who was still known as Abram at the time) do?

> And he believed in the Lord, and He accounted it to him for righteousness. (Genesis 15:6).

Abraham believed what God promised.

God said he would have many descendants, and even though Abraham was old and childless, he was persuaded God's promise was true.

Whatever else it may be, believing something means *being persuaded that it is true.*

Endnotes

1. http://webstersdictionary1828.com/Dictionary/Believe. Read on to see Webster's theological interpretation of what it means to believe. Accessed January 16, 2017.

2. Arndt, W., Danker, F. W., & Bauer, W.

(2000). *A Greek-English lexicon of the New Testament and other early Christian literature* (3rd ed., p. 816). Chicago: University of Chicago Press.

People, Things, or Propositions?

I RECENTLY SAW a T-Shirt that read, "I'd like to grow my own food, but I couldn't find any bacon seeds."

Obviously, bacon isn't the kind of thing you can grow from seed, and if you're planting a garden, you need to learn what kinds of food grow from seed.

Likewise, if you're going to understand what it means to believe, you need to know what kinds of things you can believe.

In other words, what can be the object of faith?

Our definition of faith already points to an answer. If believing means being *persuaded that something is true,* and not believing means being *persuaded that something is false,* then the object of our faith must be the kind of thing *that can be*

either true or false. But what might those be?
Let's consider some options.

Physical Objects

First, how about physical objects? Can they be true or false?

For example, can chunks of granite, Indian Motorcycles, or acoustic guitars be true or false? Can you believe them?

If someone said, "That chunk of granite is true," would that make any sense? How about if I said, "That guitar is false"?

Seems not.

I suppose you could use "true" and "false" in a *metaphorical* way. You could say that a chunk of granite was "true" in the sense that it had no physical flaws, and was well suited for a building project. Or you could say a guitar was false if it was a cheap imitation of a more expensive model. But neither would be *literally* true. Physical objects have weight, height, mass, and other physical characteristics, but the concepts of *true* or *false* don't really apply to them.

Whatever the object of faith is, it doesn't seem to be physical objects.

However, *statements* about physical objects can be true or false. You could say, "That piece of granite weighs 237 lbs" or "That guitar was hand-made in America." Those statements are matter-of-fact claims that can be verified or falsified, so you can believe something about them.

Numbers and Colors

Second, what about immaterial things, like numbers and colors? Can they be true or false?

Once again those seem to be the wrong categories to apply.

You would need a wider context to believe something about numbers and colors. You would have to claim something about them, such as, "Green is a combination of blue and yellow," or "Five is an odd number." Those *claims* can be true or false, so you can believe them.

Emotions

Third, what about emotions? Can they be true or false?

Not obviously.

You can *categorize* the kind of emotion you have, e.g., you either feel anger, or sadness, or joy.

You can describe its *intensity*, e.g., "I'm furious," or "I'm mildly annoyed."

You can investigate the *reasons* for feeling a certain way, and ask yourself if the emotion is warranted, or exaggerated, or appropriate to have in a given situation. And those *reasons* might be true or false. But the emotion doesn't seem to be true or false in itself.

However, once again, you can believe statements or claims *about* your emotions, such as, "Nothing makes me happier than holding my little baby," or "I've never been more scared of an interview in my entire life."

Sensations

Fourth, what about sensations? For example, when we see the brightly lit colors of the autumn foliage, smell the smoky undertones of freshly brewed coffee, or hear the crackling of a winter fire, are those vivid sensations true or false?

No. But *propositions* about them can be. For example, the propositions, "I see two trees," or "I feel warm by this fire," *can* be either true or false, and you can believe them.

Behavior

Fifth, what about behavior? Is how we act true or false?

Once again those seem to be the wrong categories to apply to behavior in and of itself, but you could use them to describe the intentions behind a behavior. For example, you can say that someone was acting "falsely" because he pretended to be your friend, but was really planning to stab you in the back.

But behavior could only *literally* be true or false as part of a statement like, "She meant to hurt you," or "He faked his identity to max out your credit card." You can be persuaded that those propositions about behavior are either true or false.

What We Say About Things

To summarize what we've seen thus far, it seems that the concepts of *true* and *false* don't apply to physical objects, emotions, sensations, or actions, but they do apply to *statements* about all those things.

However, we shouldn't just assume that *just anything we say* can have truth value. What kind of statements can be true or false? Let's consider some options.

Questions

First, what about *questions*, such as, "Do you like your coffee black?" Is that true or false?

It seems to be neither. Your *answer* to the question can be true or false. If you say, "I like my coffee with milk," when, in fact, you hate milk, then your answer is false.

But all on their own, questions are neither true nor false. However, you can believe statements about questions.

Commands

Second, what about *commands*? If I tell my kids to "Put the dishes away," is that true or false?

Again, it seems to be neither.

However, you can say things *about* commands that are either true or false, such as who commanded it—"Daddy told me to put the dishes away"—and *that* would be true or false.

Or you could make a *judgment* about a command, such as whether it is reasonable or possible. But commands themselves are neither true nor false.

Promises

Third, what about *promises*? If someone promises he will do something, can that be true or false?

"I will pick you up at the airport," or "I will never divorce you," or "I will you give you eternal life."

Can they be true or false?

Yes they can.

First, a promise can be true or false depending on the *intentions* of the promise-maker. If someone intends to keep his promise, you could believe it is true. If the promise-maker has no intention of keeping it, you could believe it is false.

Second, a promise can be true or false depending on the *powers* of the promise-maker. If someone promises something they could never deliver, you can believe their promise is false.

Third, a promise can be true or false depending on the *character* of the promise-maker. If an untrustworthy person makes you a promise, you'll likely not believe it. On the other hand, if he is trustworthy, with a track record of keeping his promises, you will.

Fourth, a promise can be true or false *after the fact*, depending on whether it was *fulfilled*. If someone promised to pay you back on Friday, and then didn't, that promise would be a lie, and you could believe it was false.

So, you *can* believe a promise.

Propositions

Not just everything we say is true or false. The kinds of statements that can be true or false seem to be *propositions*. As Gordon H. Clark said, "A proposition...is defined as the meaning of a declarative sentence."[1]

Hence, the objects of our faith—the things we are persuaded of being either true or false—are propositions.

Faith is propositional.

I know that's a fancy word you've probably never used. I'm sure my little French grandmother has never used it and she's believed in Jesus almost her whole life. However, she's told me to believe many propositions (even if she didn't know that's what they were), such as: "My Shawn, if you go outside in the cold with wet hair, you'll die of pneumonia!"

That's a proposition. It's a claim about reality. (In this case, it's a false claim, but it's a claim all the same.)

Here's how Webster's 1828 defines a proposition:

> "(1) That which is proposed; that which is offered for consideration, acceptance or adoption; a proposal; offer of terms...(4)... any thing stated or affirmed for discussion or illustration."[2]

A proposition is not a physical thing you can measure, weigh, or study under a microscope. It is a *statement,* a declarative sentence that asserts something about something else. It is made up of words that form a meaningful sentence "offered for consideration, acceptance or adoption," which you think about. If someone tells you, "George Washington was the first President of the United States," or "Canada is north of Mexico," or "Cats are better than dogs," what do you "do" with those propositions? They're not the kind of things you can hold in your hand, but you can think about them with your mind.

It's the same with faith.

Believing is not something you do with your

body, but with your mind. Someone tells you that "Canada is north of Mexico" and you *think* about what the proposition means. You weigh the evidence for and against it, you consider other possibilities, and ultimately, you come to a conclusion about whether it is true or false. You're either persuaded in your mind that the proposition is true, or you aren't.

That's what faith is.

Endnotes

1. Gordon H. Clark, *Logic* (Unicoi, TN: The Trinity Foundation, 1985), 28.

2. http://webstersdictionary1828.com/Dictionary/proposition. Accessed January 16, 2017.

APPENDIX 3

The Saving Proposition

WHAT DO YOU need to believe to be saved? If having faith means believing that a proposition is true, what is the saving proposition?

Quite frankly, many pastors and theologians aren't sure.

They believe we are saved by faith, apart from works, but don't know *what* you're supposed to have faith *in*.

For example, Louis Berkhof didn't know: "It is impossible to determine with precision just how much knowledge is absolutely required in saving faith."[1]

Gordon H. Clark wasn't sure, either. On the one hand, he denied there was any single saving message: "the idea of a minimum faith must be dropped as unbiblical."[2] On the other hand, Clark believed there were many propositions that must be believed in order to be saved: "There seems to be no other conclusion but that God justifies sinners by means of many combinations of propositions believed."[3] The problem was, he wasn't sure what those propositions were, so he counselled preachers to preach the whole Bible in the hopes that people would eventually believe the right combination of propositions and be saved.[4]

If you believe that you are saved by faith apart from works, but aren't sure what the saving message is, you'll never be sure that you've met the condition of salvation. Instead of assurance, you'll have doubt.

Would God really emphasize salvation by faith alone, and then not tell you what to have faith in? Would God really want His children to be perpetually uncertain about the saving message? Would he really want them to doubt whether they are saved?

Does that seem sensible to you?

I don't think so. In fact, I know it's not true because God has made the saving message very clear in John's Gospel.

The Message of Life

The saving message—the saving proposition you must believe to spend eternity with God—*is Jesus' promise of everlasting life.*

As you read these promises, I want you to think in terms of *condition* and *consequence*. Ask yourself: what's the *condition* that I must meet? And what is the *consequence* if I meet the condition?

> "Most assuredly, I say to you, he who believes in Me has everlasting life" (John 6:47).

> For God so loved the world that He gave His only begotten Son, that whoever believes in Him should not perish but have everlasting life (John 3:16).

> "He who believes in the Son has everlasting life; and he who does not believe the Son shall not see life, but the wrath of God abides on him" (John 3:36).

> "For it is My Father's will that everyone who looks to the Son and believes in Him shall have eternal life, and I will raise him up at the last day" (John 6:40, NIV).

So, what is the *condition* you find in these promises? Is it going to church? Giving money to the poor? Saying prayers? Getting baptized? Being a generally good person?

No.

So what is it?

Believe.

Specifically, *believe in the Son.*

And what's the consequence of believing?

Good karma? A chance at salvation? Strength to pull yourself up by your own bootstraps?

No.

So what is it?

You have everlasting life.

So if you put those two elements together—both the condition with the consequence—what do you get?

If you believe in the Son, you have everlasting life.

That's the saving proposition, or the saving message. That's what you must believe in order to be saved.

Simple, isn't it?

If you believe that, you have saving faith. If you don't believe it, you don't have saving faith. And if you've never believed it, then you've never had saving faith.

You see, there aren't different *kinds* of faith, but only different *objects* of faith. There aren't different *ways* of believing, but different *propositions* we believe.

Faith is saving when you believe the saving proposition. In other words, you have saving faith *when you believe in Jesus for everlasting life.*

Getting the Concepts Right

Jesus' language is so simple. When we do evangelism, we should use the words that He used. Even children can understand it. Believe in Him and you will have everlasting life.

However, most preachers have not used Jesus' words and have left multitudes confused.

Now, technically speaking, you don't need to believe in those exact words in order to be saved. What you need to believe is the *meaning* of Jesus' promise, not necessarily His *exact wording*. (But if we know the exact wording, why not use it?)

So, for example, in Montreal (where I grew up), when I came to faith, it wasn't by believing the "eternal life" language of John's Gospel, but by believing Paul's message about justification through faith in Jesus, apart from works. That's a saving message, too. If you believe that, you are saved.

Someone else might believe in Jesus in order to "go to heaven forever," or he might believe in Jesus for "once saved, always saved," or to "be with God" after he dies. Or as I tell my little kids, we believe in Jesus for "forever life."

Communicating the exact terminology isn't as important as communicating the meaning of the promise. What meaning is that?

First, that we are saved *by believing*, not by working. Salvation is by faith alone, not faith plus something else.

Second, we believe in Jesus *for everlasting life.* Salvation cannot be lost. It's forever. You can't get it one day, and then lose it the next. God promises eternal security, not probation.

Third, salvation is by believing *in Jesus.* Not Allah. Not Joseph Smith. Not Mary, the Pope, or any other guru, holy person, or generic deity. Salvation is by believing in Jesus Christ. He is the Way, the Truth, and the Life. He died on the cross as an atonement for sin, and rose again from the dead, to make salvation possible. He is the Messiah—the Christ, the Savior. He is the one who makes the promise, and He is the one we believe for eternal life. Saving faith is faith in Jesus.

Put those together and you have the saving proposition.

What About You?

Have you believed the saving proposition?

Have you believed that saving message?

If you have ever believed in Jesus for life that lasts forever—whatever terms you used to communicate those truths—then you believed the saving message and are saved forever.

You have everlasting life.

That's what Jesus promised.

Yes, eternal life is dynamic. It has qualitative aspects to it. You can have it more or less abundantly. Eternal life can grow and develop and has future aspects to it (e.g., our future resurrection, glorification, and life in the Kingdom). But it starts the moment you first believed in Jesus for it.

Do you believe that?

Endnotes

1. Louis Berkhof, *Systematic Theology*, 4th Edition (Grand Rapids, MI: Eerdmans, 1939, 1981), 504.

2. Gordon H. Clark, *Today's Evangelism: Counterfeit or Genuine?* (Jefferson, MD: The Trinity Foundation, 1990), 67.

3. Gordon H. Clark, *Faith and Saving Faith* (Jefferson, MD: The Trinity Foundaion, 1990), 110.

4. Ibid., 110.

The Assuring Proposition

"OF COURSE, I believe in Jesus," Fr. Paisius said. He was an Orthodox priest and we were discussing the condition of eternal salvation.

"And so, you're sure that you're saved?" I asked.

"Well, no one can be sure of that, but I have every hope that I will be."

"On what basis?"

"That God is merciful. He'll have mercy on me, a poor sinner, and see that I tried my best to be faithful."

"Do you ever doubt that you'll be saved?"

"Doesn't everyone?"

The priest lacked assurance. In his particular case, it was because he believed in salvation by works, not Jesus' promise of everlasting life.

But he was typical of many Evangelicals I've met. They insist they believe in Jesus, while also insisting they aren't sure if they're saved. The question was—what did they believe in Jesus for? In Fr. Paisius's case, he believed in Jesus for a chance to save himself, by doing his best to be faithful in this life. Naturally, he lacked assurance.

Likewise, many Evangelicals have believed in Jesus for *something*. But for what? That isn't always clear.

Actually, the fact that many of these Evangelicals lack assurance of salvation indicates they have not believed in Jesus for what He has actually promised.

You see, assurance is of the essence of saving faith. What that means, is that you are assured of what you believe to be true. If you believe the saving message you must have assurance of your salvation. And if you don't have assurance, it's because you either do not understand, or do not believe, the saving message. You may believe something about Jesus, but not what He promised.

Assurance Is Belief

What is assurance? It is not a feeling, emotion, or experience (although assurance can be attended by all those things). Instead, assurance is a *belief*. Being assured and being persuaded are synonyms. If you are assured that something is true, you are persuaded that it is true. It makes no sense to say that you are persuaded that something is true, and yet have no assurance about it, unless you're defining assurance as, say, a form of emotion.

What, then, is assurance of salvation? It is the belief that, "I have everlasting life." If you are persuaded that you have everlasting life, then you have assurance of salvation. That's all it is. Simple, right?

Of course, you don't need to believe *those exact words* to have assurance. Instead, you could believe, "I will go to heaven when I die," or "I will spend forever with God," or "I am saved" or the equivalent. If you believed any of those propositions, you would be assured of your salvation.

The big question is, how do you reach the conclusion that you have everlasting life? What is it based on?

That's where the syllogism comes in.

A Simple Deduction

Do you remember studying simple logic in high school? The first thing you might have learned was the deductive syllogism. Here's a classic example:

P1: All men are mortal.
P2: Socrates is a man.

C: Therefore, Socrates is mortal.

You take one premise (e.g., "All men are mortal"), add a second (e.g., "Socrates is a man"), and then draw the necessary conclusion (e.g., "Socrates is mortal").

It's the simplest form of logical thinking, the kind we use every day, often without realizing it.

You can think about assurance as a deductive syllogism in which the conclusion is, "Therefore, I have everlasting life." But if that's the conclusion, what are the premises it is based on?

The Practical Syllogism

When it comes to assurance, Calvinist and Arminian theologians teach the so-called *practical syllogism*. Their syllogism is "practical" because it bases assurance on your practical behavior.

Here's how it works.

The first premise of the practical syllogism is some standard of behavior that regenerate people are expected to live up to.

The second premise comes from observing your behavior to see if you have met the standard.

You then draw the appropriate conclusion based on those premises. Usually they look for negative behavior. For example,

P1: No regenerate person commits adultery.

P2: I commit adultery.

C: Therefore, I am not regenerate.

The problem is, there are usually many different standards of being regenerate, and even if you live up to one, chances are you'll fail in another. You might not commit adultery, but do you get angry, jealous, doubtful, envious, or covetous? You might not be a murderer, but have you really loved the people around you, including your enemies?

With such mixed results, how can you know if you're really regenerate?

You can't.

And what's worse, even if you meet a standard now, there's no guarantee you'll meet it in the future. You don't know what the future holds—you might end up committing adultery. In which case, that would prove you weren't really regenerate to begin with.

In other words, the practical syllogism is never grounds for *assurance* of salvation. If anything, it is grounds for *doubting* your salvation.

The Assurance Syllogism

By contrast, consider what I'm calling the assurance syllogism. It's based on faith in Jesus' promise, not on observing our standards of behavior.

We can see the assurance syllogism at work in John 11:25-27, in which Jesus spoke to Martha about the message of life. He said to her,

> "I am the resurrection and the life. He who believes in Me, though he may die, he shall live. And whoever lives and believes in Me shall never die. Do you believe this?" She said to Him, "Yes, Lord, I believe that You are the Christ, the Son of God, who is to come into the world."

Throughout the Gospel of John, Jesus had several ways of presenting the promise of life. In this case, given the death of Lazarus, and Martha's request that Jesus raise him from the dead, the Lord evangelized Martha by speaking about the future resurrection of believers, and saying that whoever believes in Him "will never die." Of course, if you can *never die*, that means you have *everlasting life*, which is the term Jesus most often uses (cf. John 3:15-16, 36; 5:24; 6:35, 40; 11:25-26).

Let's take that promise as the first premise in our syllogism.

I want to emphasize how important this move is. As Miles J. Stanford once said, "Unless our faith is established upon facts, it is no more than conjecture, superstition, or presumption."[1] Your assurance of salvation must be based on bedrock, not sand. And nothing is firmer than Jesus' promise of life. Now what's the second premise?

The Second Premise

Next, Jesus asked Martha a simple question— "Do you believe this?" This is the question everyone must answer when presented with Jesus' message of life. Do you believe it?

Martha could have given three different answers: "I don't believe," or "I don't know if I believe," or "I do believe." Each answer can be taken as the second premise in our syllogism. And each would lead to a different conclusion.

Let's consider each one in turn.

Three Possibilities

Let's imagine that Martha answered, "I don't believe." What conclusion would she come to?

P1: Whoever believes in Jesus has everlasting life.
P2: I don't believe.
C: Therefore, I don't have everlasting life.

If Martha concluded, "I don't have everlasting life," she would obviously not have assurance of salvation. At least, not based on Jesus' promise. She might have assurance based on other grounds (a possibility I'll discuss later), but it would not be based on believing Jesus' promise of life.

Many people have that same problem today. They lack assurance because while they may believe different facts about Jesus, they don't believe in His promise of life.

Of course, Martha could have answered, "*I don't know* if I believe." That would have led her to this conclusion:

P1: Whoever believes in Jesus has everlasting life.
P2: I don't know if I believe.
C: Therefore, I don't know if I have everlasting life.

Of course, if you don't know you have everlasting life, then you lack assurance.

(And notice that whether you disbelieve or doubt Jesus' promise the result is the same—no assurance).

But what did Martha actually answer? "Yes, Lord, I believe." She believed what He said! She had faith in Him. She believed Jesus was the Messiah who would guarantee her everlasting life simply by believing in Him for it. As soon as Martha gave that answer, she could conclude:

P1: Whoever believes in Jesus has everlasting life.
P2: I believe.
C: Therefore, I have everlasting life.

If Martha believed "I have everlasting life,"

based on believing Jesus' promise, she would have been assured of her salvation. And her assurance would have been genuine.

That's the assurance syllogism in a nutshell.

Unlike the practical syllogism, it is based on faith in Jesus' promise, not on our works.

If you believe Jesus' promise, you should reach the same conclusion, and be sure of your salvation.

The Essence of Saving Faith

If you're not sure of your salvation, but claim to believe in Jesus' promise, maybe you don't really understand what Jesus said.

The Lord promised that everlasting life is the *present possession* of believers. "He who believes *has* everlasting life," the Lord said (John 6:47, emphasis added). Has. That's present tense.

So, if you know that Jesus gives everlasting life to believers as a present possession, and you believe that promise, then what do you have as a present possession?

Everlasting life.

You know you have everlasting life right now, as a present possession, because that's what you're believing in Him for. And if you believe you have everlasting life as a present possession then you have assurance of salvation.

In other words, you cannot believe Jesus'

promise without being assured of your salvation. Assurance is the essence of saving faith, *because it is built into Jesus' promise of everlasting life.*

For example, imagine if I promised you, "I just put $100 in your pocket." Now, are you sure you have $100 in your pocket? Well it depends on whether you believe me or not. If you believe me, you'll be sure. If you don't, you won't.

Likewise, with assurance of salvation. If you believe Jesus, you'll be sure. If you don't, you won't.

Now, if Jesus had promised that believers could only have the *possibility* of gaining everlasting life *sometime in the future,* then lack of assurance would be built into His promise. You could hope to be saved, but you couldn't be sure of it. With that kind of promise, assurance wouldn't be the essence of saving faith.

But the fact is, assurance is built into Jesus' promise. The Lord said *that believers have everlasting life.* If you consider yourself a believer who has faith in that promise, then you must believe you have everlasting life as a present possession. And if you believe that, you have assurance.

False Assurance

Of course, not everyone who believes "I have everlasting life" actually has it. There is such a thing as false assurance. There are many people—

maybe millions and billions—who are sure they're going to spend eternity with God, but who aren't born again.

So what's the difference between genuine assurance and false assurance?

Once again, if you think in terms of a simple syllogism, the difference is obvious.

While genuine assurance is based on believing *a true premise* (i.e., Jesus' promise of everlasting life), false assurance is based on believing *a false premise*. Here are some examples of what I mean.

First, false assurance can come from believing in a false god. So, for example, a Muslim might reason like this:

P1: Allah will save those who die in jihad.
P2: I will die in jihad.
C: Therefore, I will be saved.

This syllogism is valid, but not sound. It is valid because the conclusion follows logically from the premises. But it is not sound, because the premises are false. A Muslim who believes that conclusion will have assurance of salvation, but it would be false assurance because Allah does not exist and no one will be saved by murdering people.

Second, false assurance can come from believing a false gospel. For example:

P1: God will save everyone who is baptized as a child.

P2: I was baptized as a child.

C: Therefore, I will be saved.

People who believe in salvation by works (such as baptism) often have assurance of salvation, but it is false assurance because no one is saved on the basis of works (Romans 3:20; Galatians 2:16).

Third, false assurance can be based on mystical experiences (the "mystical syllogism"). For example:

P1: Whoever has felt a burning in the bosom is saved.

P2: I felt a burning in my bosom.

C: Therefore, I am saved.

If someone's assurance is based on a mystical experience, it would be false assurance, because the Bible does not base assurance on fleeting experiences and emotions.

In order for a conclusion to be true, the premises must be true. In the case of assurance, the only genuine basis to conclude that you have everlasting life, is to believe in Jesus' promise.

Conclusion

What does it mean to be assured of your

salvation? It simply means believing, "I have everlasting life." If you believe that, then you have assurance. And if you believe that based on Jesus' promise of everlasting life, your assurance is genuine.

If you're doubting your salvation, it's probably because you don't understand Jesus' promise, or you don't believe it. In which case, I suggest you read over the promise of life and think of it as a simple syllogism.

Jesus promised everlasting life as a present possession to believers. If you consider yourself a believer, and you believe Jesus' promise, *then what do you have right now?*

Endnotes

1. Miles J. Stanford, *The Green Letters: Principles of Spiritual Growth* (Grand Rapids, MI: Zondervan, 1975), 9.

If you came to believe in Jesus for eternal life or gained assurance of your salvation through reading my book, I would really like to hear your story. Please write to me at:

Shawn Lazar
c/o Grace Evangelical Society
PO BOX 1308
Denton, TX 76202

And if you would like more information about assurance, the message of life, or how to grow as a follower of Jesus, please visit faithalone.org and sign up for a free subscription to *Grace in Focus* magazine. We want to continue to be a blessing to you.

Warmly,

Scripture Index

Subject Index

Shawn Lazar is the Editor of *Grace in Focus* magazine and Director of Publications for Grace Evangelical Society.

Shawn was born and raised in Montreal, Canada, and has been a proud US citizen since 2013.

He has a BTh from McGill University and an MA from the Free University, Amsterdam, with further studies conducted at Gordon-Conwell Theological Seminary, the Baptist Missionary Association Theological Seminary, and Kellogg College, University of Oxford.

Shawn and his wife Abby, together with their three children, Daphne, Zane, and Scout, make their home in Denton, TX.

GRACE IN FOCUS is a free, bimonthly magazine about the gospel, assurance, and related issues.

You will read powerful testimonies, insightful Biblical studies, and encouraging practical lessons on living for Christ.

You will especially be presented with a clear saving message of faith alone, in Christ alone, for everlasting life that cannot be lost.

For your free U.S. subscription sign up at www.faithalone.org or send your name and address to P.O. Box 1308, Denton, TX 76202.

Six Secrets of the Christian Life by Zane C. Hodges.

How do you live the Christian life? By working hard at it? By firmly making up your mind to do it? In this short book, Hodges sets forth some basic principles for growing in Christ. Now with study questions.

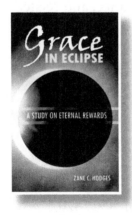

Grace in Eclipse: A Study on Eternal Rewards by Zane C. Hodges

In this timely work, Zane Hodges presents an exegetically oriented treatise on the doctrine of rewards and their relationship to the gospel. Through a careful analysis of the pertinent passages of Scripture, he argues conclusively that the believer's faithfulness or unfaithfulness to the cause of Christ in this life will result in both rewards and regrets in the life hereafter.

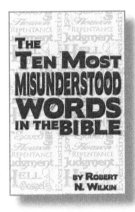

The Ten Most Misunderstood Words in the Bible by Bob Wilkin.

Words are the building blocks of ideas. Without words, we could not communicate accurately. While all the words in the Bible are important for us to understand, some stand out as being especially important. The ten words discussed in this book are foundational to our eternal destinies and our eternal well-being.

The Grace New Testament Commentary explains all of the difficult texts, including some that seem to deny eternal security, or that seem to contradict justification by faith alone, or that seem to condition kingdom entrance upon perseverance.

What Is Grace Evangelical Society?

Grace Evangelical Society (GES), founded in 1986, seeks to focus worldwide attention on the distinction between the freeness of eternal life and the costliness of eternal rewards until Jesus returns. GES provides many ways to help you grow in your faith:

- A free bimonthly magazine
- A semiannual journal
- Commentaries
- Books and booklets
- Audio and video messages
- Seminars and conferences

www.faithalone.org

Made in the USA
Middletown, DE
20 May 2023